A 52-Week Guided Journey of
Faith, Scripture & Devotionals for
Our Precious Grandchildren

Prayer journal
— FOR —
GRANDPARENTS

Julie & Jeffrey
McDonnell

This Journal Belongs To

_____

Creating Our Own Light, LLC

Copyright ©2024 Julie and Jeffrey McDonnell

Published by Creating Our Own Light (COOL) Books
P.O. Box 44 High Ridge, MO 63049

For details or ordering information, contact the publisher at support@ourcoollife.com.

All rights reserved. No part of this publication may be reproduced or transmitted in any form or by any means, electronic or mechanical, including photocopy, recording, or any information storage and retrieval system, without permission in writing from the publisher.

All Scripture quotations, unless otherwise indicated, are taken from the Holy Bible, New International Version®, NIV®. Copyright ©1973, 1978, 1984, 2011 by Biblica, Inc.™ Used by permission of Zondervan. All rights reserved worldwide. www.zondervan.com The "NIV" and "New International Version" are trademarks registered in the United States Patent and Trademark Office by Biblica, Inc.™

ISBN: 979-8-9910546-8-3

Chat GPT 4 and Grammarly Artificial Intelligence (AI) tools were utilized to assist in research, grammar, spelling, and punctuation in the creation of this journal.

*To our precious Angel granddaughter in heaven,
Camille Mae, and her amazing siblings,
Nadia Rose and Callan Michael.*

*You inspire us each day in your unique ways and
are the catalysts for this journal. Thank you for
activating God in our hearts each day.*

Mimi and PopPop Love You Very Much!

Table of Contents

Welcome Letter .... **7 - 8**

About the Journal .... **9 - 18**

Faith & Miracles .... **20 - 57**
- † Week 1 .... 21 - 24
- † Week 2 .... 25 - 28
- † Week 3 .... 29 - 32
- † Week 4 .... 33 - 36
- † Week 5 .... 37 - 40
- † Week 6 .... 41 - 44
- † Week 7 .... 45 - 48
- † Week 8 .... 49 - 52
- † Week 9 .... 53 - 56

Love & Comfort .... **58 - 95**
- † Week 10 .... 59 - 62
- † Week 11 .... 63 - 66
- † Week 12 .... 67 - 70
- † Week 13 .... 71 - 74
- † Week 14 .... 75 - 78
- † Week 15 .... 79 - 82
- † Week 16 .... 83 - 86
- † Week 17 .... 87 - 90
- † Week 18 .... 91 - 94

Joy & Wonder .... **96 - 133**
- † Week 19 .... 97 - 100
- † Week 20 .... 101 - 104
- † Week 21 .... 105 - 108
- † Week 22 .... 109 - 112
- † Week 23 .... 113 - 116
- † Week 24 .... 117 - 120
- † Week 25 .... 121 - 124
- † Week 26 .... 125 - 128
- † Week 27 .... 129 - 132

Table of Contents

Gratitude & Praise .... 134 - 167
- † Week 28................. 135 - 138
- † Week 29................. 139 - 142
- † Week 30................. 143 - 146
- † Week 31................. 147 - 150
- † Week 32................. 151 - 154
- † Week 33................. 155 - 158
- † Week 34................. 159 - 162
- † Week 35................. 163 - 166

Grace & Forgiveness .... 168 - 205
- † Week 36................. 169 - 172
- † Week 37................. 173 - 176
- † Week 38................. 177 - 180
- † Week 39................. 181 - 184
- † Week 40................. 185 - 188
- † Week 41................. 189 - 192
- † Week 42................. 193 - 196
- † Week 43................. 197 - 200
- † Week 44................. 201 - 204

Wisdom & Purpose .... 206 - 239
- † Week 45 .... 207 - 210
- † Week 46................. 211 - 214
- † Week 47................. 215 - 218
- † Week 48................. 219 - 222
- † Week 49................. 223 - 226
- † Week 50................. 227 - 230
- † Week 51................. 231 - 234
- † Week 52................. 235 - 238

My Prayers .... 240 - 250
About the Authors 251
Upcoming Books................. 252

A Welcome Letter from the Authors

Dear Beloved Grandparents,

We welcome you to this sacred journey of faith, family, and the transformative Power of Prayer. We open our hearts to you with joy and gratitude for joining us in this Divine connection for and with our precious grandchildren.

Through this 52-week journey, our intention is for you to find not only a collection of inspired prayers and related Bible verses but also a living and breathing guide for connecting you and your loved ones to the Divine through prayer.

The creation of this journal was initiated by pain, loss, and the profound impact of prayer in our personal lives. Our granddaughter Camille, a perfect Angel, went to Heaven during the final stages of our daughter Jessica's twin pregnancy now over 4 years ago.

We lost Camille, but we were fortunate enough to have her twin sister and our loving granddaughter, Nadia, survive. She is still very much connected with Camille. We know our dear Angel is always with us!

In the depths of grief for losing Camille, we turned to prayer, finding solace and strength that transcended our pain. Through this challenging journey, Jeffrey received a Divine calling to share the sacred space of prayer with others.

Guided by a profound connection with Jesus, Jeffrey opened his heart and was inspired to share the prayers you will experience in this journal. This collection of prayers, Bible verses, and reflection prompts have been created from love, not only for our cherished grandchildren, Nadia, Callan, and our Angel Camille, but for all who seek peace, healing, and connection with the Divine through the practice of prayer.

A Welcome Letter from the Authors

As proud parents, loving grandparents, and caregivers during our grandchildren's formative years, we cherish the importance of being with those we love. Family lies at the heart of our journey, and spending time with our children and grandchildren is our greatest joy. Jeffrey, affectionately known as "PopPop," and Julie, lovingly referred to as "Mimi," are grateful for every moment on this earth with Nadia and Callan.

We know some of you cannot connect directly with your grandchildren regularly. That could be because of distance or a disconnect within the family dynamic. If this journal is used consistently and with the right intention, these prayers and reflection prompts will help you stay connected!

Prayers transcend time and space. They offer the most profound Divine connection for you and those you love. They offer support and healing regardless of the proximity or awareness of those receiving the prayers.

We hope this journal becomes a Divine light for you and all grandparents worldwide, fostering deeper connections with our respective grandchildren and nurturing them in faith, love, and prosperity. Through our shared commitment to faith, family, and the incredible Power of Prayer, we welcome you wholeheartedly to this journey, which we believe will enrich the written words and touch the very core of you and your loved one's Spirit.

May the prayers within these pages provide comfort, strength, and connection on your spiritual journey. May they also bring you even closer to your precious grandchildren. They are always in our prayers!

With all the joy and love in our hearts,

Julie and Jeffrey

About this Journal

There are 6 themes with 8 to 9 prayers each, totaling 52 weeks of prayers and reflections.

Your prayer Journal consists of 4 different sections:

Inspired Prayer

Bible Reflection

Journaling (Reflect, Express, Act, & Praise)

My Prayers

This journal is designed for you to go through the **Inspired Prayer**, **Bible Reflection**, and **Journaling** sections one week at a time, starting in **Week 1** and ending in **Week 52**. Each prayer and theme has been designed in a specific order to elevate your year-long journey.

The following pages will explain each of these areas in detail so you can get started quickly and benefit from using the journal to connect with the Divine and support your grandchildren.

Inspired Prayer

Jeffrey has been blessed with the gift of connecting with the Divine (God, Father, Creator, Universe, etc.) and allowing inspired words to flow through him that positively impact others. These moments of inspiration are captured, recorded, and transcribed in this journal's "Inspired Prayers" section, designed for weekly reflection.

The term "inspiration" might hold different meanings for different people. For us, being inspired is being "In Spirit" and is a profoundly personal and spiritual experience where we connect with the Divine through prayer and meditation. This connection enables us to become vessels for wisdom, healing, and insights.

For your prayer time, we recommend finding a quiet place where you will not be interrupted or distracted. We suggest you try to block out at least 30 minutes one day or more a week for your prayers and reflections.

Each week (52 total) features a new Inspired Prayer for reflection and meditation. This will assist in opening your heart to the Divine and your grandchildren.

Week 1 Prayer

Inspired Prayer

Heavenly Creator,

I am here in prayer for my grandchildren. I come to You to guide them to Your ever-steadfast, loving space in their hearts.

Our hearts can sometimes be shadowed by shame, guilt, anger, or fear. When they face life's challenges, guide them to Your heart, the place where there is always forgiveness, grace, understanding, and compassion.

We often struggle to extend compassion to ourselves, to forgive our failings. Hidden behind our shame and guilt, we build walls from others' eyes, afraid to reveal our vulnerability and authenticity. Yet, You always see and know us as we truly are.

I pray that now and throughout their lives, You grant them the strength, grace, and faith to bring their burdens to You, forgive themselves, release their shame, guilt, anger, fear, and worries, and entrust them to Your care.

Guide them, Lord. Show them the path to true forgiveness, grace, and peace. Bestow upon them and those they touch the gift of transformation.

With all my love and light, in Your name, Your son Jesus Christ and the Holy Spirit.

Amen

Inspired Prayer

Each prayer is associated with a theme. The Inspired Prayers and Bible Verse Reflections have six themes.

- ❖ Faith & Miracles
- ❖ Love & Comfort
- ❖ Joy & Wonder
- ❖ Gratitude & Praise
- ❖ Grace & Forgiveness
- ❖ Wisdom & Purpose

Once settled in a comfortable and quiet place, read aloud the "Inspired Prayer" for the week. You are welcome to alter the words of the prayer as you see fit. For example, we often use the word God or Father as an alternative to the terms Divine or Creator. An essential aspect of prayer is using words that resonate and are meaningful for you.

If you need to read and speak the prayer multiple times, please do so! We promise you will know when your heart is open and connected. When the Divine fills your heart, it is unmistakable and typically brings waves of sensations and emotions, such as peace, joy, and gratitude.

Once you feel connected to the energy of the Divine, take as much time as you need to reflect on your thoughts, emotions, feelings, and desires. It is not the time to journal just yet. You are in listening mode! The next step is to go to the source of the Creator's words, which is the "Bible Reflection" for the week.

Our hope for this journal is that Jeffrey's prayers inspire you each week and activate your highest intentions. We firmly believe heart-centered prayer opens a pathway to Divine love and inspiration for the world.

Bible Reflection

We regard the Bible as a foundational source of Divine wisdom, moral guidance, and spiritual nourishment. Each week, we have included two Bible verses inspired by the Inspired Prayer in the "Weekly Bible Verses" section of the Journal. Engaging deeply with these scriptures will strengthen your faith and provide timely insight and guidance for you and your grandchildren.

We encourage you to read each verse out loud with focused intention and then use the reflection prompts to meditate on the Creator's words as they relate to you and your grandchildren's lives at this moment. Let this time be a continued listening exercise to hear the Divine speaking to and through you. Once you feel inspired, it is then time to start the "Journaling" process.

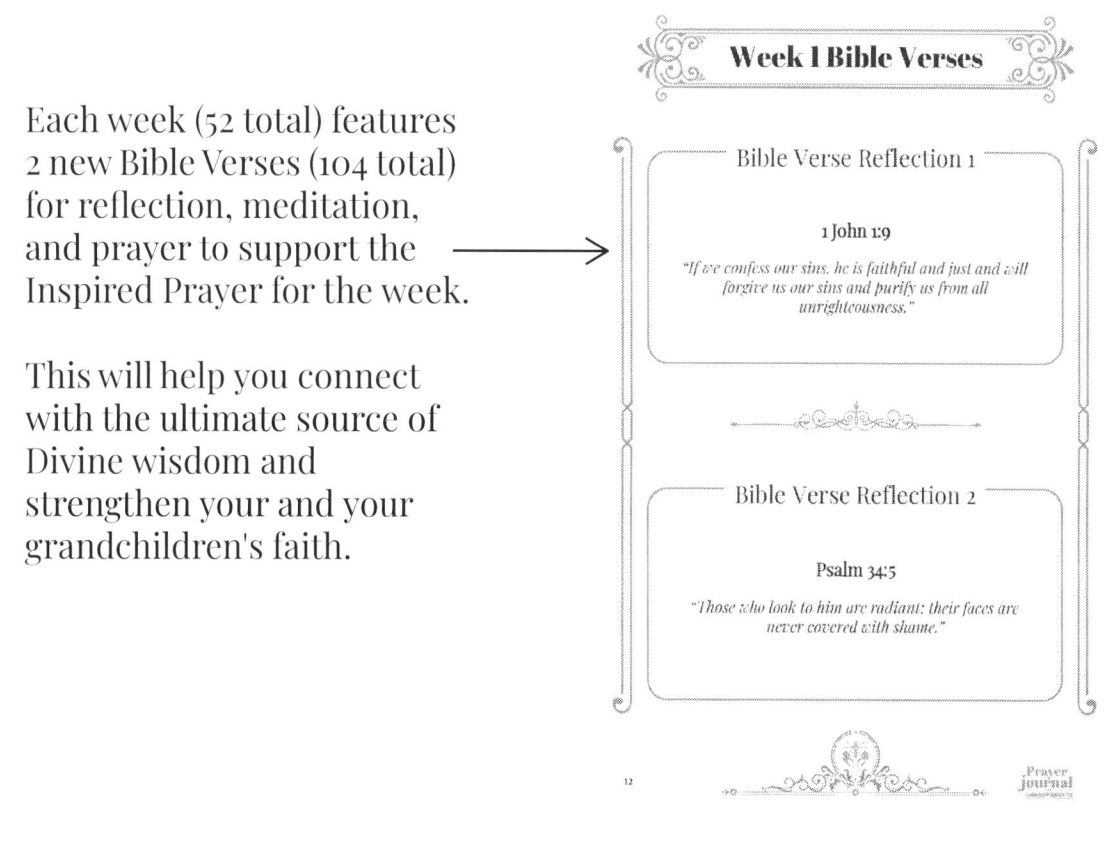

Each week (52 total) features 2 new Bible Verses (104 total) for reflection, meditation, and prayer to support the Inspired Prayer for the week.

This will help you connect with the ultimate source of Divine wisdom and strengthen your and your grandchildren's faith.

Week 1 Bible Verses

Bible Verse Reflection 1

1 John 1:9

"If we confess our sins, he is faithful and just and will forgive us our sins and purify us from all unrighteousness."

Bible Verse Reflection 2

Psalm 34:5

"Those who look to him are radiant; their faces are never covered with shame."

Journaling

As the Bible states in **Galatians 6:7**, *"Do not be deceived: God cannot be mocked. A man reaps what he sows."* One technique to sow our desires and intentions is focused prayer supported by journaling.

Having a structured framework for prayer and journaling is incredibly valuable. Committing our thoughts and reflections to paper often brings clarity and perspective, enriching our spiritual life. We believe the primary purpose of prayer is to develop a meaningful and personal relationship with the Creator, characterized by honest and open two-way communication.

Prayer involves speaking to the Divine, while journaling is about listening and reflecting on how the Divine communicates with and through us. This understanding led us to create the concept of **REAP**—**R**eflect, **E**xpress, **A**ct, and **P**raise.

Reflect, Express, Act, & Praise (REAP)

The first step is to **Reflect** by journaling the thoughts, feelings, and emotions the Divine has placed in your heart and mind. The second step is to **Express** your experiences and understanding to the Divine. The third step involves **Act**ing on the Divine inspiration you received by sharing your desires, wishes, and intentions through heart-centered prayer. The final step is to **Praise** the Creator, confident in the knowledge that prayers from the heart and for the highest good are already manifest, as stated in **John 15:7**.

"If you remain in me and my words remain in you, ask whatever you wish, and it will be done for you."

Each week, we provide four prompts for the Inspired Prayers and Bible Reflections, corresponding to each step of the **REAP** process. Below, we have included example responses for each prompt and guidance on where to record these in the journal.

Journaling
Reflect & Express

Reflect

Prompt:
This prayer and associated bible verses have opened my heart to be grateful for...

Example Response:
"Lord, thank You for touching my heart and for showing me how special my grandchildren are to me. Thank You for bringing out the child-like wonder and play in my life through them."

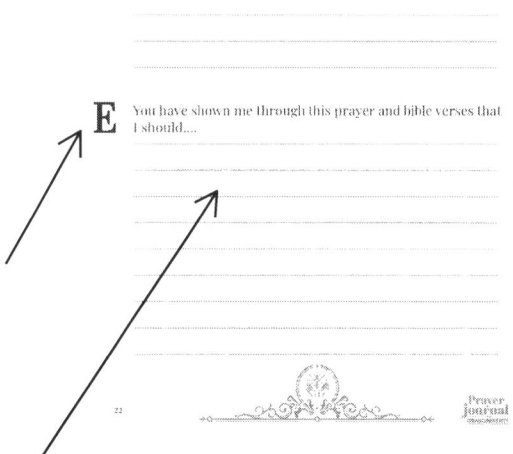

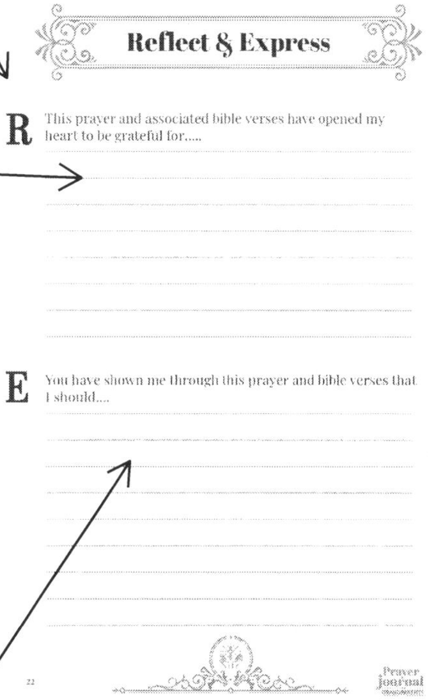

Express

Prompt:
You have shown me through this Inspired Prayer and Bible Verses that....

Example Response:
"You have shown me that I desire to be more present with my grandchildren. And that I want to have the energy to play more and experience this beautiful world You have created."

Journaling
Act & Praise

Act

Prompt:

I pray for my grandchildren and myself to....

Example Response:

"Lord, I pray for more time, health, energy, and inspiration each day to play and experience new things in this world with my grandchildren. Guide me to be their inspiration and to show them all the ways You grace this earth with Your love and abundance."

Praise

Prompt:

I know Your Divine will is manifest, and my prayers are answered. I praise and give thanks for... (write and state each prayer above as an affirmation)

Example Response:

"I am so grateful, Lord, for Your gift of health, energy, vitality, and presence. I am so blessed I have the vitality to be present with my grandchildren and that You so graciously use me as a vessel to show them Your never-ending love."

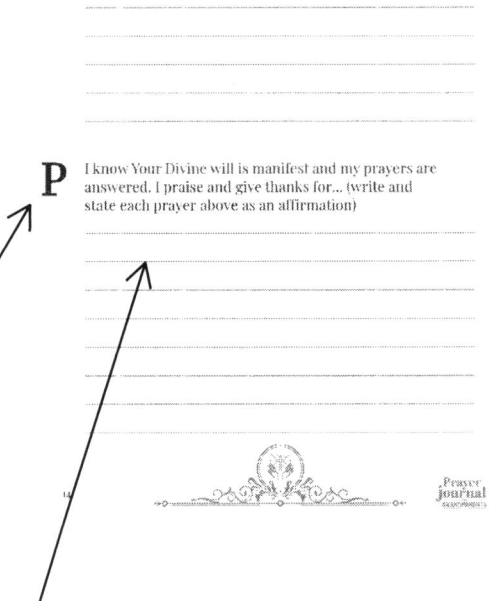

My Prayers

Starting on **Page 240**, this section documents your prayers and assists you in the art of manifestation. You can enter up to two prayers per page. It is crucial to follow up regularly and review your prayers every 3 to 6 months to see how they have been answered. Often, we set our intentions and pray earnestly but fail to recognize when the Divine has responded.

Start by documenting the date of each prayer and detailing your intentions as clearly as possible. Then, release your expectations, and trust your prayer will be fulfilled if it is true to your heart and for the highest good of all.

After 3 to 6 months, revisit your journal to review your prayers. For any prayer that has been answered, note the date it was manifested and add any personal reflections. It's okay if you need help remembering the exact date. Recognizing your prayers have been answered is a cause for celebration and a vital ingredient in strengthening your relationship with the Divine!

You might also find prayers that were significant to you when you entered them in the journal but have yet to manifest and no longer resonate. This is a beautiful opportunity to expand your awareness and discern what aligns with your Spirit.

Reflect on what has changed in your perception or situation. Maybe what you prayed for was not actually what you needed, or the answer came unexpectedly and more profoundly. Often, the Divine surprises us, revealing deeper truths within our hearts.

My Prayers

Prayer

Enter the Date of Your Prayer

Enter Your Prayer Request

Date Manifested

Review every 3 to 6 months and mark the date when your prayer was answered or when you recognized it no longer resonates in your heart.

Personal Note

Write any reflections or notes about the prayer and how it was answered. This process will help develop your trust and awareness in Divine timing. Over time, you will realize how much the universe completely loves and supports you.

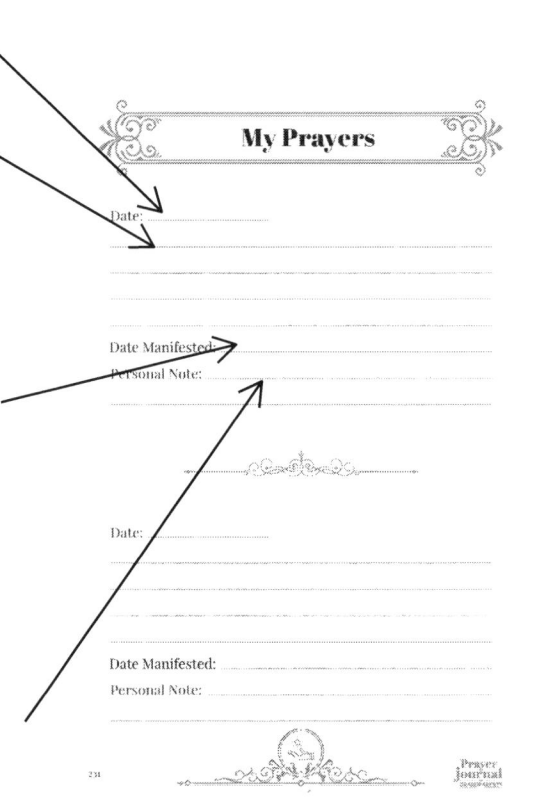

Getting Started

We hope you find the journal prompts and the example responses helpful to guide you. If this approach to journaling does not resonate with you, please feel free to follow your intuition on how you want to best utilize the Inspired Prayers and Bible Verses in this journal. We have blank journal pages that are freely available for download and printing on our website at **OurCOOLLife.com**.

Even though we designed the journal to follow the weekly prayers and themes in order, we encourage you to utilize it in any way that works best. Feel empowered to do what calls your heart the most! We have found that being at ease and in flow is the key to elevating your prayer and journaling time.

Writing down your thoughts can sometimes feel challenging if you are new to journaling. We encourage you to follow the prompts and give it a few weeks before giving up, as most people find it easier the more they journal.

After a few weeks, if you still find it difficult to write down your thoughts, we suggest verbalizing them and recording them with a smartphone, tablet, or audio recording device. For some, speaking is much easier than writing. For other tips and tools to use while journaling, please visit our website at **OurCOOLLife.com**.

"An act of Faith precedes every Miracle."

Jeffrey and Julie McDonnell

Faith & Miracles

Week 1 Prayer

Inspired Prayer

Heavenly Creator,

I am here in prayer for my grandchildren. I come to You to guide them to Your ever-steadfast, loving space in their hearts.

Our hearts can sometimes be shadowed by shame, guilt, anger, or fear. When they face life's challenges, guide them to Your heart, the place where there is always forgiveness, grace, understanding, and compassion.

We often struggle to extend compassion to ourselves, to forgive our failings. Hidden behind our shame and guilt, we build walls from others' eyes, afraid to reveal our vulnerability and authenticity. Yet, You always see and know us as we truly are.

I pray that now and throughout their lives, You grant them the strength, grace, and faith to bring their burdens to You, forgive themselves, release their shame, guilt, anger, fear, and worries, and entrust them to Your care.

Guide them, Lord. Show them the path to true forgiveness, grace, and peace. Bestow upon them and those they touch the gift of transformation.

With all my love and light, in Your name, Your son Jesus Christ and the Holy Spirit.

Amen

Week 1 Bible Verses

Bible Verse Reflection 1

1 John 1:9

"If we confess our sins, he is faithful and just and will forgive us our sins and purify us from all unrighteousness."

Bible Verse Reflection 2

Psalm 34:5

"Those who look to him are radiant; their faces are never covered with shame."

Reflect & Express

R This prayer and associated bible verses have opened my heart to be grateful for...

_____
_____
_____
_____
_____
_____
_____
_____

E You have shown me through this prayer and bible verses that...

_____
_____
_____
_____
_____
_____
_____
_____
_____

Act & Praise

A I pray for my grandchildren and myself to...

P I know Your Divine will is manifest, and my prayers are answered. I praise and give thanks for.... (write and state each prayer above as an affirmation)

Week 2 Prayer

Inspired Prayer

Divine Creator,

Today, I lift up my grandchildren in prayer, opening my heart and being fully in Your presence.

In this moment, I focus my loving thoughts on them, asking for Your blessings.

May Your grace, peace, and love envelop them, filling them with a sense of awe and wonder at Your creation.

Illuminate their eyes with excitement and joy, guiding them to learn, grow, and interact with the world through Your essence.

May they reflect Your light, letting their eyes sparkle like angels, and their voices sing with the freedom and joy of Your creation.

Though I may not be physically with them now, they are forever in my heart, as I am in theirs.

Thank You, Lord, for the blessing of their presence in my life.

Amen

Week 2 Bible Verses

Bible Verse Reflection 1

Psalm 127:3

"Children are a heritage from the Lord, offspring a reward from him."

Bible Verse Reflection 2

1 John 3:18

"Dear children, let us not love with words or speech but with actions and in truth."

Reflect & Express

R This prayer and associated bible verses have opened my heart to be grateful for...

_____

_____

_____

_____

_____

_____

_____

E You have shown me through this prayer and bible verses that...

_____

_____

_____

_____

_____

_____

_____

_____

Act & Praise

A I pray for my grandchildren and myself to...

P I know Your Divine will is manifest, and my prayers are answered. I praise and give thanks for.... (write and state each prayer above as an affirmation)

Week 3 Prayer

Inspired Prayer

Divine Creator,

Open my heart, mind, and being to Your presence.

In moments when I resist receiving or giving love, guide me.

Please help me be fully present with my grandchildren, embrace them, and give them all of myself.

Allow me to let go of worries and fears, becoming an open pathway for them to express Your light.

Grant me the grace and humility to discern the truth in all things, the truth that reflects You.

In Your Name, in Your Son Jesus Christ's Name, and the Holy Spirit, I pray,

Amen

Week 3 Bible Verses

Bible Verse Reflection 1

Philippians 4:6-7

"Do not be anxious about anything, but in every situation, by prayer and petition, with thanksgiving, present your requests to God. And the peace of God, which transcends all understanding, will guard your hearts and your minds in Christ Jesus."

Bible Verse Reflection 2

Ezekiel 36:26

"I will give you a new heart and put a new spirit in you; I will remove from you your heart of stone and give you a heart of flesh."

Reflect & Express

R This prayer and associated bible verses have opened my heart to be grateful for...

E You have shown me through this prayer and bible verses that...

Act & Praise

A I pray for my grandchildren and myself to…

P I know Your Divine will is manifest, and my prayers are answered. I praise and give thanks for…. (write and state each prayer above as an affirmation)

Week 4 Prayer

Inspired Prayer

Heavenly Creator,

May my grandchildren express themselves uniquely and beautifully. Please help us to listen, see, and embrace them, especially in their frustrations.

Guide them not to suppress their emotions or conform against their true selves. Let them feel, acknowledge, and see Your presence in their emotions, for therein lies Your truth and love.

Grant them the ability to find Your peace amidst anger and feel Your love when unnoticed. Assure them of Your constant presence. Inspire them to open their hearts to love more, to see more, and to extend compassion to others, even in times of anger and hurt.

I know You recognize me in every aspect, Lord. Please bestow this understanding upon my grandchildren. Let them immerse themselves in this awareness and express everything through this knowledge. I trust Your greatest love lies in our most significant challenges.

With all my love, light, peace, and presence, I pray in Your Name, Your Son Jesus' Name, and the Holy Spirit.

Amen

Week 4 Bible Verses

Bible Verse Reflection 1

Isaiah 41:10

"So do not fear, for I am with you; do not be dismayed, for I am your God. I will strengthen you and help you; I will uphold you with my righteous right hand."

Bible Verse Reflection 2

2 Corinthians 1:3-4

"Praise be to the God and Father of our Lord Jesus Christ, the Father of compassion and the God of all comfort, who comforts us in all our troubles, so that we can comfort those in any trouble with the comfort we ourselves receive from God."

Reflect & Express

R This prayer and associated bible verses have opened my heart to be grateful for…

E You have shown me through this prayer and bible verses that…

Act & Praise

A I pray for my grandchildren and myself to...

P I know Your Divine will is manifest, and my prayers are answered. I praise and give thanks for.... (write and state each prayer above as an affirmation)

Week 5 Prayer

Inspired Prayer

Divine Creator,

Open my eyes, ears, mind, heart, and being to Your essence. Guide me, Lord.

I am grateful for being filled with Your presence, embraced by Your love and acceptance.

Envelop my grandchildren with Your magnificent energy. May they feel Your presence daily. Fill them with the joy I have experienced, and let them hear the angels sing praises to You.

Infuse their souls with light, allowing them to express Your love in this world. May they carry the heart of Jesus in their earthly journey.

In joyful and challenging times, may they always perceive Your presence as a comfort in times of worries, fears, and struggles. It is a special blessing I wish for my children and grandchildren. Grant them this gift, Lord. Through me, let them see Your desires for them.

With all my love and light, in this moment and always, in Your Name and in all that is love, in Your Son Jesus' Name, and the Holy Spirit.

Amen

Week 5 Bible Verses

Bible Verse Reflection 1

Psalm 23:4

"Even though I walk through the darkest valley, I will fear no evil, for you are with me; your rod and your staff, they comfort me."

Bible Verse Reflection 2

John 14:27

"Peace I leave with you; my peace I give you. I do not give to you as the world gives. Do not let your hearts be troubled and do not be afraid."

Reflect & Express

R This prayer and associated bible verses have opened my heart to be grateful for...

_____
_____
_____
_____
_____
_____
_____

E You have shown me through this prayer and bible verses that...

_____
_____
_____
_____
_____
_____
_____
_____

Act & Praise

A I pray for my grandchildren and myself to...

P I know Your Divine will is manifest, and my prayers are answered. I praise and give thanks for.... (write and state each prayer above as an affirmation)

Week 6 Prayer

Inspired Prayer

Divine Creator,

Open my heart, mind, ears, and eyes to Your Divine presence.

Bless my grandchildren, connecting them with the earth and allowing Your energy to flow through them, reaching the heavens.

As they raise their hands in praise, may they feel deeply connected to the earth in Your Name.

Lord, let Your light and healing power be manifest on this earth through us.

Guide my grandchildren in prayer, in recognizing Your constant presence, and in reflecting Your light.

May they always remember they are Your cherished creations.

In Your Name, Your Son Jesus' Name, and the Holy Spirit, we embrace Your gifts of love, grace, peace, and presence.

With all my love!

Amen

Week 6 Bible Verses

Bible Verse Reflection 1

Ephesians 1:18

"I pray that the eyes of your heart may be enlightened in order that you may know the hope to which he has called you, the riches of his glorious inheritance in his holy people."

Bible Verse Reflection 2

Deuteronomy 31:6

"Be strong and courageous. Do not be afraid or terrified because of them, for the LORD your God goes with you; he will never leave you nor forsake you."

Reflect & Express

R This prayer and associated bible verses have opened my heart to be grateful for...

_____
_____
_____
_____
_____
_____
_____

E You have shown me through this prayer and bible verses that...

_____
_____
_____
_____
_____
_____
_____
_____

Act & Praise

A   I pray for my grandchildren and myself to…

P   I know Your Divine will is manifest, and my prayers are answered. I praise and give thanks for…. (write and state each prayer above as an affirmation)

Week 7 Prayer

Inspired Prayer

Divine Creator,

Open my heart, mind, and being to Your essence. Guide me in Your love, peace, and presence, now and always.

May my grandchildren see Your miracles in themselves and their lives.

Help them speak their truth, recognizing healing, health, and vibrancy are gifts from Your light of love and grace.

Beneath the world's noise, let them feel and be anchored in this truth.

We seek Your support, Father, to be their ever-present foundation.

May Your Son, Jesus, walk with them daily. Let the Holy Spirit illuminate them each morning, bringing joy to their days in the light of the world.

Thank You!

We pray in Your name, Your Son Jesus Christ, and the Holy Spirit.

Amen

Week 7 Bible Verses

Bible Verse Reflection 1

Psalm 107:20

"He sent out his word and healed them; he rescued them from the grave."

Bible Verse Reflection 2

John 8:32

"Then you will know the truth, and the truth will set you free."

Reflect & Express

R This prayer and associated bible verses have opened my heart to be grateful for...

_____
_____
_____
_____
_____
_____
_____

E You have shown me through this prayer and bible verses that...

_____
_____
_____
_____
_____
_____
_____
_____
_____

Act & Praise

A I pray for my grandchildren and myself to…

P I know Your Divine will is manifest, and my prayers are answered. I praise and give thanks for…. (write and state each prayer above as an affirmation)

Week 8 Prayer

Inspired Prayer

Heavenly Creator,

Open our hearts, minds, and beings to Your presence.

Guide us with Your love, light, peace, grace, and constant presence.

Today and every day, grant peace to my beloved grandchildren.

Let them revel in Your love and joy and dance in Your embrace beneath the sun.

Teach us to breathe in Your essence, to see Your spirit in their smiles and bright eyes.

Protect and guide them, Lord, showing them Your ways.

I pray their hearts continue to grow in Your love, spreading Your boundless generosity across the earth.

Thank You, Lord, for my grandchildren, this profound love, and Your unwavering presence in our lives.

Amen

Week 8 Bible Verses

Bible Verse Reflection 1

Psalm 119:105

"Your word is a lamp for my feet, a light on my path."

Bible Verse Reflection 2

Psalm 121:7-8

"The LORD will keep you from all harm— He will watch over your life; the LORD will watch over your coming and going both now and forevermore."

Reflect & Express

R This prayer and associated bible verses have opened my heart to be grateful for...

_____
_____
_____
_____
_____
_____
_____

E You have shown me through this prayer and bible verses that...

_____
_____
_____
_____
_____
_____
_____
_____

Act & Praise

A I pray for my grandchildren and myself to...

P I know Your Divine will is manifest, and my prayers are answered. I praise and give thanks for.... (write and state each prayer above as an affirmation)

Week 9 Prayer

Inspired Prayer

Heavenly Creator,

I open my heart, mind, and being to You. Guide me with Your love, light, peace, and presence.

Lead me in the path of Your Son, Jesus Christ, and the Holy Spirit.

Today, I pray for my grandchildren. May they come to know and experience true faith in You.

Grant them a solid foundation to find peace, joy, and love in Your presence. Help them recognize Your guidance within them.

May they wholeheartedly turn to You, Lord, especially in challenging times.

Let them feel Your presence during life's storms and see Your glory in nature's beauty.

Bless their parents with the joy of nurturing and loving them. Remind them of Your everlasting care and love. Be their Rock, now and always.

With all my love and light, I pray in Your name, Lord, in Jesus' name, in the Holy Spirit.

Amen

Week 9 Bible Verses

Bible Verse Reflection 1

Hebrews 11:1

"Now faith is confidence in what we hope for and assurance about what we do not see."

Bible Verse Reflection 2

Proverbs 22:6

"Start children off on the way they should go, and even when they are old they will not turn from it."

Reflect & Express

R This prayer and associated bible verses have opened my heart to be grateful for...

_____
_____
_____
_____
_____
_____
_____

E You have shown me through this prayer and bible verses that...

_____
_____
_____
_____
_____
_____
_____
_____

Act & Praise

A I pray for my grandchildren and myself to...

P I know Your Divine will is manifest, and my prayers are answered. I praise and give thanks for.... (write and state each prayer above as an affirmation)

"*God loves You as You are today; there is nothing You need to change.*"

Jeffrey McDonnell

Love & Comfort

Week 10 Prayer

Inspired Prayer

Divine Creator,

I offer You my heartfelt request for my grandchildren. I pray they are wrapped in Your love and nurture the presence of joy, peace, and grace in their hearts.

Guide them to understand the power of forgiveness, the beauty of acceptance, and the joy of expression. Teach them the warmth of love, the comfort of hugs, and the brightness of smiles.

May the light in their eyes shine brightly, illuminating the path for others to see and feel Your presence. Let Your love radiate through them, touching everyone they encounter.

As they go through life, inspire them to live filled with Your Spirit, marked by infinite acceptance, love, creativity, and expansion.

When they encounter fear or uncertainty, let them find solace in You. May they connect with the Holy Spirit each morning, breathing in Your love and energy and expressing it into the world.

Amen

Week 10 Bible Verses

Bible Verse Reflection 1

Deuteronomy 11:18-19

"Fix these words of mine in your hearts and minds; tie them as symbols on your hands and bind them on your foreheads. Teach them to your children, talking about them when you sit at home and when you walk along the road, when you lie down and when you get up."

Bible Verse Reflection 2

Romans 8:26

"In the same way, the Spirit helps us in our weakness. We do not know what we ought to pray for, but the Spirit himself intercedes for us through wordless groans."

Reflect & Express

R This prayer and associated bible verses have opened my heart to be grateful for...

_____
_____
_____
_____
_____
_____
_____

E You have shown me through this prayer and bible verses that...

_____
_____
_____
_____
_____
_____
_____
_____

Act & Praise

A I pray for my grandchildren and myself to...

P I know Your Divine will is manifest, and my prayers are answered. I praise and give thanks for.... (write and state each prayer above as an affirmation)

Week 11 Prayer

Inspired Prayer

Divine Creator,

Today, I offer my prayers, seeking peace for my grandchildren.

May they experience Your presence in their hearts, feeling seen, embraced, and known by Your loving touch.

I sense Your closeness in the joy of playing with them, in their laughter, and the sparkle in their eyes.

Grant through my heartbeat, my breath, my patience, and my words, they may feel Your peace.

May the light of Your love shine through me, guiding them all their days.

Let them understand the depth of Your peace and love—unconditional and ever-welcoming—through my embrace.

Amen

Week 11 Bible Verses

Bible Verse Reflection 1

1 John 4:12

"No one has ever seen God; but if we love one another, God lives in us and his love is made complete in us."

Bible Verse Reflection 2

Psalm 29:11

"The LORD gives strength to his people; the LORD blesses his people with peace."

Reflect & Express

R This prayer and associated bible verses have opened my heart to be grateful for...

_____
_____
_____
_____
_____
_____
_____

E You have shown me through this prayer and bible verses that...

_____
_____
_____
_____
_____
_____
_____
_____

Act & Praise

A I pray for my grandchildren and myself to...

P I know Your Divine will is manifest, and my prayers are answered. I praise and give thanks for.... (write and state each prayer above as an affirmation)

Week 12 Prayer

Inspired Prayer

Divine Creator,

Open my grandchildren's hearts to perceive Your love in all its forms – to see, feel, and hear it in everything around them.

Help them understand the truth they are whole, complete, and acknowledged for their true selves.

They are created in Your image, Lord, which is divinely perfect in all ways.

May they feel embraced and cradled in Your love, Lord, fully accepting the beauty of who they are and see their true nature through Your eyes.

In Your name, the name of Jesus Christ, Your Son, and the Holy Spirit,

Amen

Week 12 Bible Verses

Bible Verse Reflection 1

Psalm 139:14

"I praise You because I am fearfully and wonderfully made; Your works are wonderful, I know that full well."

Bible Verse Reflection 2

Psalm 139:1-3

"You have searched me, LORD, and You know me. You know when I sit and when I rise; You perceive my thoughts from afar. You discern my going out and my lying down; You are familiar with all my ways."

Reflect & Express

R This prayer and associated bible verses have opened my heart to be grateful for...

_____
_____
_____
_____
_____
_____
_____

E You have shown me through this prayer and bible verses that...

_____
_____
_____
_____
_____
_____
_____
_____

Act & Praise

A I pray for my grandchildren and myself to...

_____
_____
_____
_____
_____
_____
_____

P I know Your Divine will is manifest, and my prayers are answered. I praise and give thanks for.... (write and state each prayer above as an affirmation)

_____
_____
_____
_____
_____
_____
_____
_____

Week 13 Prayer

Inspired Prayer

Heavenly Creator of all that exists,

Open my heart and mind. Make me a vessel for Your love—a love that is unconditional, nonjudgmental, complete, and all-encompassing.

May this love embrace my grandchildren, letting them feel Your presence.

Let Your light shine through me, illuminating their path as Your children.

Let them find safety, wholeness, visibility, and a voice in my arms.

Free from me all that does not align with Your will so I may better reflect Your Divine nature to my grandchildren.

In Your name, Your Son Jesus Christ's name, and the Holy Spirit. I pray.

Amen

Week 13 Bible Verses

Bible Verse Reflection 1

Romans 8:38-39

"For I am convinced that neither death nor life, neither angels nor demons, neither the present nor the future, nor any powers, neither height nor depth nor anything else in all creation, will be able to separate us from the love of God that is in Christ Jesus our Lord."

Bible Verse Reflection 2

2 Timothy 2:21

"Those who cleanse themselves from the latter will be instruments for special purposes, made holy, useful to the Master and prepared to do any good work."

Reflect & Express

R This prayer and associated bible verses have opened my heart to be grateful for…

_____
_____
_____
_____
_____
_____
_____

E You have shown me through this prayer and bible verses that…

_____
_____
_____
_____
_____
_____
_____
_____

Act & Praise

A I pray for my grandchildren and myself to…

P I know Your Divine will is manifest, and my prayers are answered. I praise and give thanks for…. (write and state each prayer above as an affirmation)

Week 14 Prayer

Inspired Prayer

Divine Creator,

At this moment, I humbly ask to be fully present with my grandchildren.

Grant me the grace to listen to them, to truly see them, to embrace them, and to love them without condition.

Please help me cherish their laughter and uplift their dreams and hopes.

Please make me a trusted refuge for them, especially when life doesn't go as planned.

Allow me to be Your voice, Your eyes, Your ears, and Your heart for them here on earth.

Remind them of how precious they are to You and the universe.

I am profoundly grateful for the gift and opportunity of being a grandparent.

Thank You, Lord, for these blessings. With all my love and gratitude,

Amen

Week 14 Bible Verses

Bible Verse Reflection 1

1 Corinthians 13:4-7

"Love is patient, love is kind. It does not envy, it does not boast, it is not proud. It does not dishonor others, it is not self-seeking, it is not easily angered, it keeps no record of wrongs. Love does not delight in evil but rejoices with the truth. It always protects, always trusts, always hopes, always perseveres."

Bible Verse Reflection 2

1 Peter 4:8

"Above all, love each other deeply, because love covers over a multitude of sins."

Reflect & Express

R This prayer and associated bible verses have opened my heart to be grateful for...

_____
_____
_____
_____
_____
_____

E You have shown me through this prayer and bible verses that...

_____
_____
_____
_____
_____
_____
_____

Act & Praise

A   I pray for my grandchildren and myself to...

P   I know Your Divine will is manifest, and my prayers are answered. I praise and give thanks for.... (write and state each prayer above as an affirmation)

Week 15 Prayer

Inspired Prayer

Heavenly Creator, breathe into me today.

I miss my grandchildren deeply. The joy of spending time with them makes their absence more profound.

Today, I pray for a day filled with Your love, where their parents see them fully, embracing them with the warmth and complete acceptance of Your love.

May they reflect Your grace, love, and presence to everyone they meet.

My love is always with them. I eagerly anticipate our next embrace, our time together, and the simple joy of having fun with them, which fills my heart.

Thank You, Lord, for this deep yearning, a longing for the essence of You.

Fill me with Your spirit, guide me, and grant me Your peace and presence in all things.

Let me await our next meeting with the eagerness of a child, longing for the day I can hold them in my arms again.

I pray in Your Name, in Your Son Jesus Christ's Name, and the Holy Spirit,

Amen

Week 15 Bible Verses

Bible Verse Reflection 1

Isaiah 58:11

"The Lord will guide you always; he will satisfy your needs in a sun-scorched land and will strengthen your frame. You will be like a well-watered garden, like a spring whose waters never fail."

Bible Verse Reflection 2

Psalm 42:1-2

"As the deer pants for streams of water, so my soul pants for You, my God. My soul thirsts for God, for the living God. When can I go and meet with God?"

Reflect & Express

R This prayer and associated bible verses have opened my heart to be grateful for...

E You have shown me through this prayer and bible verses that...

Act & Praise

A I pray for my grandchildren and myself to...

P I know Your Divine will is manifest, and my prayers are answered. I praise and give thanks for.... (write and state each prayer above as an affirmation)

Week 16 Prayer

Inspired Prayer

Divine Creator,

Open my heart, eyes, ears, and being to Your presence.

I seek a deeper connection with You, Lord, so my grandchildren may also connect with You, sensing Your love, support, and joy in their hearts.

Let me be a vessel of Your love, Lord. May the ease, flow, and grace of Your essence move through me to enrich their lives.

Help us not to erect walls against love but to receive and give love freely.

Make us fully aware of our vulnerabilities, instilling the humility needed to grow and be truly open and available for our grandchildren.

Lord, guide me to be an example for them, showing how to walk in Your footsteps.

I pray in Your Name, Your Son Jesus' Name, and the Holy Spirit, now and forever.

Amen

Week 16 Bible Verses

Bible Verse Reflection 1

Deuteronomy 6:6-7

"These commandments that I give you today are to be on your hearts. Impress them on your children. Talk about them when you sit at home and when you walk along the road, when you lie down and when you get up."

Bible Verse Reflection 2

Ephesians 5:1-2

"Follow God's example, therefore, as dearly loved children and walk in the way of love, just as Christ loved us and gave himself up for us as a fragrant offering and sacrifice to God."

Reflect & Express

R This prayer and associated bible verses have opened my heart to be grateful for...

_____
_____
_____
_____
_____
_____
_____

E You have shown me through this prayer and bible verses that...

_____
_____
_____
_____
_____
_____
_____
_____

Act & Praise

A   I pray for my grandchildren and myself to...

_____

_____

_____

_____

_____

_____

P   I know Your Divine will is manifest, and my prayers are answered. I praise and give thanks for.... (write and state each prayer above as an affirmation)

_____

_____

_____

_____

_____

_____

Week 17 Prayer

Inspired Prayer

Heavenly Creator and all that is,

I ask for Your guidance to open my eyes, ears, mind, heart, and all my senses to Your Divine presence. Lead me with Your love, light, peace, and grace.

At this moment, I ask for Your presence with me in prayer for my cherished grandchildren.

Lord, bless them with the awareness of love's importance, both in giving and receiving. May they understand the preciousness of being with loved ones and be open to the love surrounding them.

Help me to express my love for them as freely and unconditionally as You have shown me. Through Your grace, may they feel Your love channeling through me.

Grant them the joy of experiencing life fully – to dance to the music, to sing joyfully, and to love their siblings, parents, and all around them. Let them be receptive to love and nurture from others.

I am deeply grateful, Lord, for Your constant presence and for hearing my prayers. Thank You for being with us in every moment.

Amen

Week 17 Bible Verses

Bible Verse Reflection 1

Psalm 107:1

"Give thanks to the Lord, for he is good; his love endures forever."

Bible Verse Reflection 2

Mark 10:14

"When Jesus saw this, he was indignant. He said to them, 'Let the little children come to me, and do not hinder them, for the kingdom of God belongs to such as these.'"

Reflect & Express

R This prayer and associated bible verses have opened my heart to be grateful for...

_____
_____
_____
_____
_____
_____
_____

E You have shown me through this prayer and bible verses that...

_____
_____
_____
_____
_____
_____
_____
_____
_____

Act & Praise

A I pray for my grandchildren and myself to…

_____

_____

_____

_____

_____

_____

_____

P I know Your Divine will is manifest, and my prayers are answered. I praise and give thanks for…. (write and state each prayer above as an affirmation)

_____

_____

_____

_____

_____

_____

_____

Week 18 Prayer

Inspired Prayer

Divine Creator,

Open my heart and mind to embrace my being and all that embodies You. Lead me with Your love, peace, patience, and grace.

Let me remain humble in Your presence. I am grateful for Your Son, Jesus Christ, and the Holy Spirit, who sustain our connection to You every moment.

Grant my grandchildren and me true contentment in knowing You deeply within our hearts. May Your presence resonate in our daily breaths, sights, and actions.

Help us not to chase the empty promises of the world but to seek the fullness and completeness that reflect our Divine nature in You.

As we face life's challenges, remind us You are always with us, guiding and supporting us. May the flow of Your energy grant us grace, peace, patience, and the wisdom to make life-enhancing decisions. When we stray, let Your inner guidance be our alert, drawing our focus back to You.

Thank You, Lord, for Your constant presence. With all my love and light, I pray in Jesus' name and the Holy Spirit,

Amen

Week 18 Bible Verses

Bible Verse Reflection 1

Psalm 46:1

"God is our refuge and strength, an ever-present help in trouble."

Bible Verse Reflection 2

Proverbs 16:3

"Commit to the LORD whatever you do, and he will establish your plans."

Reflect & Express

R This prayer and associated bible verses have opened my heart to be grateful for...

E You have shown me through this prayer and bible verses that...

Act & Praise

A I pray for my grandchildren and myself to...

P I know Your Divine will is manifest, and my prayers are answered. I praise and give thanks for.... (write and state each prayer above as an affirmation)

"Embrace life with child-like joy and wonder."

Julie McDonnell

Joy & Wonder

Week 19 Prayer

Inspired Prayer

Divine Creator,

Today, let me open my heart to my grandchildren, who are eagerly exploring the world with their eyes wide open.

As they eagerly absorb information, let them see Your presence in others.

May their smiles, laughter, and hugs be a channel of Your love, bringing more of You into this world.

Bless them with Your peace, grace, forgiveness, and presence, and let these gifts flow through them to everyone they encounter.

And, Lord, let their innocence and joy also touch my heart.

I pray in Your name, the name of Your Son Jesus Christ, and the Holy Spirit.

Amen

Week 19 Bible Verses

Bible Verse Reflection 1

Matthew 18:3

"And he said: 'Truly I tell you, unless you change and become like little children, you will never enter the kingdom of heaven.'"

Bible Verse Reflection 2

Numbers 6:24-26

"'The LORD bless you and keep you; the LORD make his face shine on you and be gracious to you; the LORD turn his face toward you and give you peace."

Reflect & Express

R This prayer and associated bible verses have opened my heart to be grateful for...

_____
_____
_____
_____
_____
_____
_____

E You have shown me through this prayer and bible verses that...

_____
_____
_____
_____
_____
_____
_____
_____

Act & Praise

A I pray for my grandchildren and myself to...

P I know Your Divine will is manifest, and my prayers are answered. I praise and give thanks for.... (write and state each prayer above as an affirmation)

Week 20 Prayer

Inspired Prayer

Heavenly Creator, source of all that is Divine and glorious,

I cherish Your presence within me, manifesting as joy, light, and exuberant energy.

May I be filled with Your spirit daily, sharing this blessing with my grandchildren.

Through me, let them witness Your light, and through them, let me see Your grace reflected.

May we bask in Your abundance, overflowing grace, and the profound joy of life and freedom in Your presence.

Help me to detach from worldly distractions, immersing myself in Your beauty, grace, and ease.

As Your energy flows through me, from my feet through my spine, I reach upwards, embracing Your warmth and vibrancy, moved to tears of joy by these Divine moments.

With heartfelt gratitude, I thank You, Lord.

Amen

Week 20 Bible Verses

Bible Verse Reflection 1

Psalm 16:11

"You make known to me the path of life; You will fill me with joy in Your presence, with eternal pleasures at Your right hand."

Bible Verse Reflection 2

Romans 12:2

"Do not conform to the pattern of this world, but be transformed by the renewing of your mind. Then you will be able to test and approve what God's will is—his good, pleasing and perfect will."

Reflect & Express

R This prayer and associated bible verses have opened my heart to be grateful for...

_____
_____
_____
_____
_____
_____
_____

E You have shown me through this prayer and bible verses that...

_____
_____
_____
_____
_____
_____
_____
_____

Act & Praise

A I pray for my grandchildren and myself to...

P I know Your Divine will is manifest, and my prayers are answered. I praise and give thanks for.... (write and state each prayer above as an affirmation)

Week 21 Prayer

Inspired Prayer

Divine Creator, the source of all that exists,

Open my eyes, ears, and heart to embrace Your presence fully.

In the beauty of this world, Lord, I see Your handiwork—in the trees, the grass, and in the joyful smile of my grandchild.

I relish the memories of the warm snuggles, the joy of storytelling, and the sweet reflections of drawing pictures on their backs with my gentle touch.

Bathe me in Your grace, Lord, and guide me to cherish and be receptive to these precious moments.

Grant me the vision to see the world through Your eyes.

In Your Name, the Name of Your Son Jesus Christ, and the Holy Spirit. I pray.

Amen

Week 21 Bible Verses

Bible Verse Reflection 1

Philippians 4:8

"Finally, brothers and sisters, whatever is true, whatever is noble, whatever is right, whatever is pure, whatever is lovely, whatever is admirable—if anything is excellent or praiseworthy—think about such things."

Bible Verse Reflection 2

Psalm 23:2-3

"He makes me lie down in green pastures, he leads me beside quiet waters, he refreshes my soul. He guides me along the right paths for his name's sake."

Reflect & Express

R This prayer and associated bible verses have opened my heart to be grateful for...

E You have shown me through this prayer and bible verses that...

Act & Praise

A   I pray for my grandchildren and myself to…

P   I know Your Divine will is manifest, and my prayers are answered. I praise and give thanks for…. (write and state each prayer above as an affirmation)

Week 22 Prayer

Inspired Prayer

Heavenly Creator,

I come to You with all that is in my heart and mind.

As I watched my grandchildren today, their smiles, playfulness, and creativity reminded me of Your profound love for us. Their joy and wonder reflect Your Divine presence.

I pray, Lord, You infuse them with a lifelong childlike spirit, guiding them to seek and find You in every aspect of their lives. May their laughter, the sparkle in their eyes when experiencing joy, and our shared moments be filled with Your spirit, reminding us of Your constant presence.

Lord, You bring ease, vibrancy, and depth to our lives. Whether in moments of joy, like watching the grandchildren have fun, or in times of frustration and challenge, we feel life more fully with You by our side.

Grant us, Lord, the grace to always sense Your presence. Let us see, feel, hear, and smell Your essence in everything.

Thank You, Lord, for Your blessings and for loving us unceasingly.

Amen

Week 22 Bible Verses

Bible Verse Reflection 1

Psalm 34:8

"Taste and see that the LORD is good; blessed is the one who takes refuge in him."

Bible Verse Reflection 2

Psalm 100:2

"Worship the Lord with gladness; come before him with joyful songs."

Reflect & Express

R This prayer and associated bible verses have opened my heart to be grateful for...

_____
_____
_____
_____
_____
_____
_____

E You have shown me through this prayer and bible verses that...

_____
_____
_____
_____
_____
_____
_____
_____

Act & Praise

A I pray for my grandchildren and myself to...

P I know Your Divine will is manifest, and my prayers are answered. I praise and give thanks for.... (write and state each prayer above as an affirmation)

Week 23 Prayer

Inspired Prayer

Divine Creator,

Open my heart, mind, and being to Your presence.

May my eyes see clearly and my heart connects deeply as I pray amidst the beauty of nature.

My heart is uplifted by my grandchildren, who find joy in the outdoors, experiencing Your creation.

May they encounter You in the rustling leaves, the playful squirrels, and the chirping birds, embracing the love that emanates from all these elements.

As they breathe in the fresh air, let them know they are worthy of Your love, allowing it to rejuvenate their spirit while they play, smile, and laugh.

Thank You, Lord, for making us conduits of Your grace, enabling us to interact with the world and perceive Your splendor in its beauty.

Help us to inhale Your essence in every moment, filled with love, light, peace, and presence.

I offer this prayer in Your Name, in Jesus' Name, and in the unity of the Holy Spirit.

Amen

Week 23 Bible Verses

Bible Verse Reflection 1

Psalm 19:1-4

"The heavens declare the glory of God; the skies proclaim the work of his hands. Day after day they pour forth speech; night after night they reveal knowledge. They have no speech, they use no words; no sound is heard from them. Yet their voice goes out into all the earth, their words to the ends of the world."

Bible Verse Reflection 2

Romans 1:20

"For since the creation of the world God's invisible qualities—his eternal power and Divine nature—have been clearly seen, being understood from what has been made, so that people are without excuse."

Reflect & Express

R This prayer and associated bible verses have opened my heart to be grateful for...

_____
_____
_____
_____
_____
_____
_____

E You have shown me through this prayer and bible verses that...

_____
_____
_____
_____
_____
_____
_____
_____
_____

Act & Praise

A I pray for my grandchildren and myself to...

P I know Your Divine will is manifest, and my prayers are answered. I praise and give thanks for.... (write and state each prayer above as an affirmation)

Week 24 Prayer

Inspired Prayer

Heavenly Creator,

Source of all that is embodied in love, light, peace, and grace.

We pray with open hearts for our beloved grandchildren.

Guide them, Lord, to trust in Your will and to live in harmony with Your Divine plan.

Help them to release any need for struggle, filling their hearts with Your boundless energy of creation, joy, and ease.

May they experience Your presence in everything, Lord – in the beauty of trees, flowers, animals, and the sounds of nature.

Bless them with a deeper understanding of their identity as Your children.

Let them breathe in Your grace, peace, and the life-giving flow of Your love.

I pray in Your Name, Lord, in the Name of Jesus Christ and the Holy Spirit, and in all that is love.

Amen

Week 24 Bible Verses

Bible Verse Reflection 1

Jeremiah 29:11

"For I know the plans I have for you,' declares the Lord, 'plans to prosper you and not to harm you, plans to give you hope and a future.'"

Bible Verse Reflection 2

Job 12:7-10

"But ask the animals, and they will teach you, or the birds in the sky, and they will tell you; or speak to the earth, and it will teach you, or let the fish in the sea inform you. Which of all these does not know that the hand of the LORD has done this? In his hand is the life of every creature and the breath of all mankind."

Reflect & Express

R This prayer and associated bible verses have opened my heart to be grateful for...

_____
_____
_____
_____
_____
_____
_____

E You have shown me through this prayer and bible verses that...

_____
_____
_____
_____
_____
_____
_____
_____
_____

Act & Praise

A I pray for my grandchildren and myself to...

P I know Your Divine will is manifest, and my prayers are answered. I praise and give thanks for.... (write and state each prayer above as an affirmation)

Week 25 Prayer

Inspired Prayer

Divine Creator,

I open my heart, mind, eyes, ears, and voice to embrace Your presence fully.

Today, my prayers are dedicated to my grandchildren. As I wandered in nature among the squirrels, chipmunks, birds, and trees, I thought of my grandchildren delighting in the beauty of the natural world.

I ask You, Lord, to reveal Your love, wonder, and astonishing grace to them. May they see Your hand in the vibrant colors of the flowers, the rustling leaves, and all the animals they encounter.

Guide them, Lord, to embrace playfulness and not shy away from getting their hands dirty or engaging in hard work—the kind of fulfilling work that brings pride and joy, feeling purposeful and rewarding.

Instill a sense of wonder in them as they observe insects, bugs, and all the earth's small creatures. Through their eyes, let them find joy and love in these experiences. Fill their hearts with a sense of play and wonder, Lord.

I offer this prayer in Your name, in the name of Jesus, and in the Holy Spirit.

Amen

Week 25 Bible Verses

Bible Verse Reflection 1

Psalm 28:7

"The LORD is my strength and my shield; my heart trusts in him, and he helps me. My heart leaps for joy, and with my song I praise him."

Bible Verse Reflection 2

Ecclesiastes 3:11

"He has made everything beautiful in its time. He has also set eternity in the human heart; yet no one can fathom what God has done from beginning to end."

Reflect & Express

R This prayer and associated bible verses have opened my heart to be grateful for...

_____
_____
_____
_____
_____
_____
_____

E You have shown me through this prayer and bible verses that...

_____
_____
_____
_____
_____
_____
_____
_____

Act & Praise

A I pray for my grandchildren and myself to...

P I know Your Divine will is manifest, and my prayers are answered. I praise and give thanks for.... (write and state each prayer above as an affirmation)

Week 26 Prayer

Inspired Prayer

Heavenly Creator,

Open my heart and mind to fully embrace You, Your Son Jesus Christ, and the Holy Spirit.

Lord, fill us with laughter, love, and joy today. Encourage us to play, jump, and sing, basking in each other's company and the delight of childhood.

May we see in our grandchildren's eyes the essence of being a child and help us all to recognize and cherish this innocence.

Protect them from losing that pure spirit, Lord.

Guide them to embrace fun, creativity, and playfulness, the qualities You envisioned at their creation.

Fill their day with love, ease, grace, and peace.

Let them dance joyfully in Your presence, their eyes sparkling with Your glory.

I offer all my love, light, peace, and presence in Your name, Lord. In Jesus' name and the Holy Spirit.

Amen

Week 26 Bible Verses

Bible Verse Reflection 1

Psalm 8:2

"Through the praise of children and infants you have established a stronghold against your enemies, to silence the foe and the avenger."

Bible Verse Reflection 2

Psalm 126:2

"Our mouths were filled with laughter, our tongues with songs of joy. Then it was said among the nations, "The LORD has done great things for them."

Reflect & Express

R This prayer and associated bible verses have opened my heart to be grateful for...

_____
_____
_____
_____
_____
_____
_____
_____

E You have shown me through this prayer and bible verses that...

_____
_____
_____
_____
_____
_____
_____
_____
_____

Act & Praise

A I pray for my grandchildren and myself to...

_____
_____
_____
_____
_____
_____
_____

P I know Your Divine will is manifest, and my prayers are answered. I praise and give thanks for.... (write and state each prayer above as an affirmation)

_____
_____
_____
_____
_____
_____
_____

Week 27 Prayer

Inspired Prayer

Divine Creator, the source of all that exists and all that will ever be.

Open my heart, mind, and being to the fullness of Your presence.

Guide me in the light of Your love as I open my heart to the joy and wonder of spending time with my grandchildren. I am continually in awe of their innocence—their unique ways of discovering the world, be it through reading a book or playing outdoors.

Their excitement and sense of wonder are truly inspiring. I pray You nurture this innate curiosity within them so they may always view life with the fresh eyes of children.

Lord, sustain their thirst for knowledge and understanding. Help them always recognize miracles in the smallest of things and cherish Your wonders in their daily lives.

May their laughter be plentiful, their excitement boundless, and their smiles ever-present. Fill their hearts with Your eternal joy.

With all my love, light, peace, and presence, I offer this prayer in Your Name, in the Name of Your Son Jesus Christ, and by the power of the Holy Spirit.

Amen

Week 27 Bible Verses

Bible Verse Reflection 1

Galatians 5:22-23

"But the fruit of the Spirit is love, joy, peace, forbearance, kindness, goodness, faithfulness, gentleness and self-control. Against such things there is no law."

Bible Verse Reflection 2

Psalm 98:4

"Shout for joy to the LORD, all the earth, burst into jubilant song with music."

Reflect & Express

R This prayer and associated bible verses have opened my heart to be grateful for...

E You have shown me through this prayer and bible verses that...

Act & Praise

A I pray for my grandchildren and myself to...

P I know Your Divine will is manifest, and my prayers are answered. I praise and give thanks for.... (write and state each prayer above as an affirmation)

"Even the smallest of God's wonders deserves Our Praise and Gratitude."

Julie McDonnell

Gratitude & Praise

Week 28 Prayer

Inspired Prayer

Heavenly Creator,

As I greet You today, I open my heart to You, inviting Your love, peace, joy, and presence to fill me, especially in my interactions with my grandchildren.

Guide me, Lord, to be fully present with them – to engage in play, to genuinely see and understand them for who they are, and to listen attentively. May I hear Your voice in their words and see Your reflection in their eyes.

Lord, grant me an open heart, free of expectations, allowing me to embrace them with the knowledge Your love illuminates them. Help me to recognize their unique specialness and the immense love they feel as they are cradled within Your arms.

I am deeply thankful, Lord, for this new day, for uplifting my heart, and for the opportunity to let the love and joy in this world be mirrored through us, Your children. My heart overflows with gratitude for my precious grandchildren.

Thank You, Lord, again and again. I pray in Your name, in the name of Jesus Christ, Your Son, and the Holy Spirit.

Amen

Week 28 Bible Verses

Bible Verse Reflection 1

Psalm 118:24

"The Lord has done it this very day; let us rejoice today and be glad."

Bible Verse Reflection 2

Psalm 143:8

"Let the morning bring me word of Your unfailing love, for I have put my trust in You. Show me the way I should go, for to You I entrust my life."

Reflect & Express

R This prayer and associated bible verses have opened my heart to be grateful for...

E You have shown me through this prayer and bible verses that...

Act & Praise

A   I pray for my grandchildren and myself to...

P   I know Your Divine will is manifest, and my prayers are answered. I praise and give thanks for.... (write and state each prayer above as an affirmation)

Week 29 Prayer

Inspired Prayer

Divine Creator,

I am deeply grateful for the way You've touched my heart today. As tears of joy well up within me, I pray their essence spills onto my beloved grandchildren, bathing them in Your light, expression, and uplifting spirit. May these tears of joy envelop every cell of their beautiful, precious being.

Lord, I am humbly aware my love for them is but a fraction of the immense love You bestow upon them.
Their every giggle, smile, and surprise they bring daily are treasures. I am in awe of Your love for them, which surpasses my understanding, a love a million times greater than mine.

I am blessed to have experienced Your presence, and I fervently pray that my grandchildren, too, will have this experience. Let them grasp and hold on to it for the rest of their lives, even if just for a moment.

Your kingdom is ever-present, Lord. It has always been among us. May Your light shine brightly and grant me the grace to play my part in this life.

I offer this prayer in Your Name, in the Name of Your Son Jesus, and the Holy Spirit.

Amen

Week 29 Bible Verses

Bible Verse Reflection 1

Psalm 100:4-5

"Enter his gates with thanksgiving and his courts with praise; give thanks to him and praise his name. For the Lord is good and his love endures forever; his faithfulness continues through all generations."

Bible Verse Reflection 2

Luke 17:21

"Nor will people say, 'Here it is,' or 'There it is,' because the kingdom of God is in your midst."

Reflect & Express

R This prayer and associated bible verses have opened my heart to be grateful for...

E You have shown me through this prayer and bible verses that...

Act & Praise

A I pray for my grandchildren and myself to...

P I know Your Divine will is manifest, and my prayers are answered. I praise and give thanks for.... (write and state each prayer above as an affirmation)

Week 30 Prayer

Inspired Prayer

Heavenly Creator,

I am deeply grateful for this time with my grandchildren, their smiles, laughter, and the joy of being youthful again.

Thank You for blessing these moments.

Help me to fully embrace and be present in these experiences, reflecting the open-hearted love You bring to the world.

May I see through Your eyes, and may Your gifts of peace, grace, joy, and radiance touch their lives as they have illuminated mine.

I pray in Your Name, in Jesus Christ's Name, and through the Holy Spirit.

Amen

Week 30 Bible Verses

Bible Verse Reflection 1

Proverbs 17:6

"Children's children are a crown to the aged, and parents are the pride of their children."

Bible Verse Reflection 2

Psalm 128:3-4

"Your wife will be like a fruitful vine within your house; your children will be like olive shoots around your table. Yes, this will be the blessing for the man who fears the LORD."

Reflect & Express

R This prayer and associated bible verses have opened my heart to be grateful for...

_____

_____

_____

_____

_____

_____

_____

E You have shown me through this prayer and bible verses that...

_____

_____

_____

_____

_____

_____

_____

_____

Act & Praise

A   I pray for my grandchildren and myself to...

P   I know Your Divine will is manifest, and my prayers are answered. I praise and give thanks for.... (write and state each prayer above as an affirmation)

Week 31 Prayer

Inspired Prayer

Divine Creator,

Today, I dedicate my time to You in gratitude. My heart overflows with thankfulness for my grandchildren—the joy of being with them, celebrating their journey as they explore the world. Their curiosity, whether they acknowledge my presence or are engrossed in their discoveries, fills me with wonder.

Though part of me yearns to spend every moment with them, I realize the importance of letting them explore independently. I see in this a reflection of Your love, Lord, how You delight in our exploration and growth, even as You remain ever-present.

I am grateful for the opportunity to observe them as a source of comfort during their frustrations. Each moment with them is a precious reminder to cherish life more deeply than I did in my youth and to appreciate the fleeting nature of time.

Lord, I am profoundly thankful for this heart full of love and for these moments that are both joyful and tender. May my smiles and my tears be an expression of my love for You.

In Your Name, Your Son Jesus' Name, and the Holy Spirit. I pray.

Amen

Week 31 Bible Verses

Bible Verse Reflection 1

Isaiah 64:8

"Yet You, Lord, are our Father. We are the clay, You are the potter; we are all the work of Your hand."

Bible Verse Reflection 2

Isaiah 40:31

"But those who hope in the LORD will renew their strength. They will soar on wings like eagles; they will run and not grow weary, they will walk and not be faint."

Reflect & Express

R This prayer and associated bible verses have opened my heart to be grateful for...

E You have shown me through this prayer and bible verses that...

Act & Praise

A I pray for my grandchildren and myself to...

P I know Your Divine will is manifest, and my prayers are answered. I praise and give thanks for.... (write and state each prayer above as an affirmation)

Week 32 Prayer

Inspired Prayer

Heavenly Creator,

Open my heart, mind, and being to embrace Your presence fully. Guide me in Your love, light, and peace.

Help me to see You in all things. Reflecting on my precious grandchildren, my heart swells with love for them—their hugs, smiles, and kisses are treasures.

I thank You, Lord, for this gift of love, the joy of embracing and laughing with them. I acknowledge how blessed I am.

Life is fragile, and each day is uncertain. Help me cherish every moment with them, holding these memories dear in my heart. Even when they are not physically with me, their essence remains vivid in my mind—a gift for which I'm immensely grateful.

Lord, let my grandchildren feel the depth of my love. Through Your grace, may they experience the beauty and love surrounding them daily. When they play, when their parents embrace them, let them feel Your presence—full of grace, beauty, peace, and patience.

With all my love and gratitude, I offer this prayer in Your name, in Jesus' name, guided by the Holy Spirit.

Amen

Week 32 Bible Verses

Bible Verse Reflection 1

James 1:17

"Every good and perfect gift is from above, coming down from the Father of the heavenly lights, who does not change like shifting shadows."

Bible Verse Reflection 2

James 4:14

"Why, you do not even know what will happen tomorrow. What is your life? You are a mist that appears for a little while and then vanishes."

Reflect & Express

R This prayer and associated bible verses have opened my heart to be grateful for...

E You have shown me through this prayer and bible verses that...

Act & Praise

A I pray for my grandchildren and myself to...

P I know Your Divine will is manifest, and my prayers are answered. I praise and give thanks for.... (write and state each prayer above as an affirmation)

Week 33 Prayer

Inspired Prayer

Divine Creator,

Open my heart, mind, and being to all that You are.

As I connect with You, Lord, I pray for the opening of doors for my grandchildren to the beauty of Your creation—the radiant balls of light, the wonders of nature, the trees, sky, birds, grass, and water.

May their eyes sparkle with Your glow and peace.
O Lord, Your heart rejoices as children play.

Let them freely express themselves, revealing the depths of who they are and the purpose You have set for them.

Guide them to seek You in all things, to find You, Lord. Hold their hands, embrace them, and breathe Your life into them. May their light shine brightly in Your glory.

I am profoundly grateful, Lord. Thank You for allowing me to see You in them every day, to feel Your presence even in my absence, and for the joy and peace I experience in their company. I know this is Your doing, Lord.

In Your Name, Your Son Jesus Christ, and the Holy Spirit. Glory to You in all things.

Amen

Week 33 Bible Verses

Bible Verse Reflection 1

Jeremiah 29:13

"You will seek me and find me when you seek me with all your heart."

Bible Verse Reflection 2

1 Thessalonians 5:16-18

"Rejoice always, pray continually, give thanks in all circumstances; for this is God's will for you in Christ Jesus."

Reflect & Express

R This prayer and associated bible verses have opened my heart to be grateful for...

E You have shown me through this prayer and bible verses that...

Act & Praise

A I pray for my grandchildren and myself to...

P I know Your Divine will is manifest, and my prayers are answered. I praise and give thanks for.... (write and state each prayer above as an affirmation)

Week 34 Prayer

Inspired Prayer

Heavenly Creator, the Divine light present in all that exists.

I open my heart, mind, eyes, ears, and soul to Your essence, to the boundless love You embody.

My heart overflows with gratitude for this day. For the cherished moments spent with my grandchildren. For the joy of their laughter and the privilege of witnessing their growth. Guide them, Lord, in learning to open their hearts to Your Divine love.

Teach them to feel Your mighty presence surging within them and elevate their spirits to offer You praise, gratitude, and honor in all aspects of life.

May their inner light reflect upon others—their family, friends, and even strangers on the street. Signal through their smiles and gazes that they are indeed Your children.

I thank You, Lord, for the abundance of Your love and the grace, peace, and illumination You provide.

I am eternally grateful for experiencing Your love through these precious souls.

Amen

Week 34 Bible Verses

Bible Verse Reflection 1

Psalm 118:1

"Give thanks to the Lord, for he is good; his love endures forever."

Bible Verse Reflection 2

2 Timothy 1:7

"For the Spirit God gave us does not make us timid, but gives us power, love and self-discipline."

Reflect & Express

R This prayer and associated bible verses have opened my heart to be grateful for...

E You have shown me through this prayer and bible verses that...

Act & Praise

A I pray for my grandchildren and myself to...

P I know Your Divine will is manifest, and my prayers are answered. I praise and give thanks for.... (write and state each prayer above as an affirmation)

Week 35 Prayer

Inspired Prayer

Heavenly Creator, the source of all that exists,

I reach out to You today with a heart full of gratitude and joy. Reflecting on my grandchildren, I am struck by the pure delight they embody.

They reignite the child within me and all whom they encounter. Witnessing their play, their laughter, their affection, their zest for life's simple pleasures — it is in these moments I truly see Your joy, love, and grace reflected in them.

Their innocence and wonder remind me to view Your creation with the same awe and marvel.

I am profoundly thankful for their presence in my life, which keeps the sense of wonder alive in my heart, whether we are together or apart. The images and videos of them keep the spirit of childlike curiosity burning bright within me.

With deep love and light that emanates from this gratitude, I offer this prayer.

In Your Divine presence, in Jesus' name, and through the Holy Spirit, I celebrate Your glory.

Amen

Week 35 Bible Verses

Bible Verse Reflection 1

Mark 10:15

"Truly I tell you, anyone who will not receive the kingdom of God like a little child will never enter it."

Bible Verse Reflection 2

Colossians 3:15-16

"Let the peace of Christ rule in your hearts, since as members of one body you were called to peace. And be thankful. Let the message of Christ dwell among you richly as you teach and admonish one another with all wisdom through psalms, hymns, and songs from the Spirit, singing to God with gratitude in your hearts."

Reflect & Express

R This prayer and associated bible verses have opened my heart to be grateful for...

_____
_____
_____
_____
_____
_____

E You have shown me through this prayer and bible verses that...

_____
_____
_____
_____
_____
_____
_____

Act & Praise

A I pray for my grandchildren and myself to...

P I know Your Divine will is manifest, and my prayers are answered. I praise and give thanks for.... (write and state each prayer above as an affirmation)

"Forgiving oneself first and then others is the doorway to the heart of Jesus."

Jeffrey McDonnell

Grace & Forgiveness

Week 36 Prayer

Inspired Prayer

Heavenly Creator,

I am here in prayer for my grandchildren. I come to You to guide them to Your ever-steadfast loving space in their hearts.

Our hearts sometimes can be shadowed by shame, guilt, anger, or fear. When they face life's challenges, guide them to Your heart—the place where there is always forgiveness, grace, understanding, and compassion.

We often struggle to extend compassion to ourselves and to forgive our failings. Hidden behind our shame and guilt, we build walls from others' eyes, afraid to reveal our vulnerability and authenticity. Yet, You always see and know us as we truly are.

I pray that you will grant them the strength, grace, and faith to bring their burdens to You, forgive themselves, release their shame, guilt, anger, fear, and worries, and entrust them to Your care now and throughout their lives.

Guide them, Lord. Show them the path to true forgiveness, grace, and peace. Bestow upon them and those they touch the gift of transformation.

With all my love and light, in Your name, Your son Jesus Christ, and the Holy Spirit.

Amen

Week 36 Bible Verses

Bible Verse Reflection 1

1 John 1:9

"If we confess our sins, he is faithful and just and will forgive us our sins and purify us from all unrighteousness."

Bible Verse Reflection 2

Psalm 34:5

"Those who look to him are radiant; their faces are never covered with shame."

Reflect & Express

R This prayer and associated bible verses have opened my heart to be grateful for…

E You have shown me through this prayer and bible verses that…

Act & Praise

A I pray for my grandchildren and myself to...

P I know Your Divine will is manifest, and my prayers are answered. I praise and give thanks for.... (write and state each prayer above as an affirmation)

Week 37 Prayer

Inspired Prayer

Heavenly Creator,

Please be present with my grandchildren today.

Reveal the depth of Your love to them, affirming their inherent worth and perfection.

Remind them your forgiveness is ever-present even when they err or feel unworthy.

Grant them the ability to forgive themselves and extend grace to others.

Help them to discern Your presence in all things.

Assure them they are never lost, for You seek them with all Your heart.

Be their constant companion, breaking through any barriers to Your love.

In Your Name, Your Son Jesus Christ, and the Holy Spirit,

Amen

Week 37 Bible Verses

Bible Verse Reflection 1

Ephesians 4:32

"Be kind and compassionate to one another, forgiving each other, just as in Christ God forgave you."

Bible Verse Reflection 2

Luke 19:10

"For the Son of Man came to seek and to save the lost."

Reflect & Express

R This prayer and associated bible verses have opened my heart to be grateful for...

E You have shown me through this prayer and bible verses that...

Act & Praise

A I pray for my grandchildren and myself to...

P I know Your Divine will is manifest, and my prayers are answered. I praise and give thanks for.... (write and state each prayer above as an affirmation)

Week 38 Prayer

Inspired Prayer

Heavenly Creator,

I ask to share Your light with the world and my grandchildren.

May Your love and grace shine brightly upon us all and give us strength.

Help us find wholeness and perfection in Your stillness, embrace, and all-knowing presence.

Open our hearts to new ways, to Your ways of being, and to finding grace even in challenging moments.

Let my grandchildren seek Your guidance, teachings, and love, especially in times of doubt.

When they ask, 'Is this God's heart? Is this the love God has for me? Is this the love God has for others?' Guide them always to choose You.

In Your Name, Your Son Jesus Christ, and the Holy Spirit,

Amen

Week 38 Bible Verses

Bible Verse Reflection 1

2 Corinthians 12:9

"But he said to me, 'My grace is sufficient for you, for my power is made perfect in weakness.' Therefore I will boast all the more gladly about my weaknesses, so that Christ's power may rest on me."

Bible Verse Reflection 2

Psalm 46:10

"He says, 'Be still, and know that I am God; I will be exalted among the nations, I will be exalted in the earth.'"

Reflect & Express

R This prayer and associated bible verses have opened my heart to be grateful for…

E You have shown me through this prayer and bible verses that…

Act & Praise

A — I pray for my grandchildren and myself to…

P — I know Your Divine will is manifest, and my prayers are answered. I praise and give thanks for…. (write and state each prayer above as an affirmation)

Week 39 Prayer

Inspired Prayer

Heavenly Creator,

We open our hearts to You.

Let us embrace Your love, grace, peace, and beauty.

Please help us see beauty in all things: in my grandchildren's eyes, smiles, and hugs, in the joy and wonder of nature, and the quiet moments of life.

Guide us away from distractions, fears, and concerns so we may remain fully present in each moment.

Instill a deep trust in Your steadfast care, filling our hearts with Your everlasting grace and abundance.

Lord, grant us Your perspective, enriching our lives with love, grace, and beauty.

We pray in Your Name, Your Son Jesus' Name, and the Holy Spirit.

Amen

Week 39 Bible Verses

Bible Verse Reflection 1

Ephesians 2:8-9

"For it is by grace you have been saved, through faith —and this not from yourselves, it is the gift of God— not by works, so that no one can boast."

Bible Verse Reflection 2

Psalm 19:1

"The heavens declare the glory of God; the skies proclaim the work of his hands."

Reflect & Express

R This prayer and associated bible verses have opened my heart to be grateful for...

_____
_____
_____
_____
_____
_____
_____

E You have shown me through this prayer and bible verse that...

_____
_____
_____
_____
_____
_____
_____

Act & Praise

A   I pray for my grandchildren and myself to...

_____
_____
_____
_____
_____
_____

P   I know Your Divine will is manifest, and my prayers are answered. I praise and give thanks for.... (write and state each prayer above as an affirmation)

_____
_____
_____
_____
_____
_____
_____

Week 40 Prayer

Inspired Prayer

Divine Creator,

Open my heart and mind to embrace Your presence fully. Please guide me in grace, patience, and peace.

Teach me the power of forgiveness, both in granting it to others and in accepting it for myself. Help me to see Your hand in all things, especially in challenging times.

I pray my grandchildren learn these lessons, too. Though I wish them no hardship, I know life brings its trials.

Grant them the strength to face these challenges, knowing Your love is with them. May they understand they carry a part of You within them, a mark of Your grace and peace, through Your Son Jesus Christ.

Bless them with innocence, wonder, joy, and the wisdom to seek forgiveness when the world seems unkind. Teach them forgiveness is not just a gift to others but a path closer to You.

With all my love and light, now and always.

I pray in Your Name, Your Son Jesus Christ, and the Holy Spirit united in Your everlasting love.

Amen

Week 40 Bible Verses

Bible Verse Reflection 1

Matthew 6:14-15

"For if you forgive other people when they sin against you, your heavenly Father will also forgive you. But if you do not forgive others their sins, your Father will not forgive your sins."

Bible Verse Reflection 2

Psalm 51:10

"Create in me a pure heart, O God, and renew a steadfast spirit within me."

Reflect & Express

R This prayer and associated bible verses have opened my heart to be grateful for...

_____

_____

_____

_____

_____

_____

E You have shown me through this prayer and bible verses that...

_____

_____

_____

_____

_____

_____

Act & Praise

A I pray for my grandchildren and myself to...

P I know Your Divine will is manifest, and my prayers are answered. I praise and give thanks for.... (write and state each prayer above as an affirmation)

Week 41 Prayer

Inspired Prayer

Heavenly Creator,

Open my heart, mind, ears, and eyes to all that is You. In this moment and every moment, guide me with Your love, light, peace, presence, and grace.

Help my grandchildren to manage their frustrations. Teach them to pause in anger and to feel Your steadying presence.

When challenges arise and emotions flare, may they remember to breathe, seek Your guidance, and approach each situation with Your grace.

Fill them with the knowledge of Your constant support and gratitude that comes from knowing You are always with them.

Let them embrace a never-ceasing prayer, feel the love in their hearts, and the love that flows through their being.

Thank You, Lord, for Your endless guidance and love.

With all my love and light, in every moment, in Your Name, Your Son Jesus' Name, and the Holy Spirit,

Amen

Week 41 Bible Verses

Bible Verse Reflection 1

James 1:19-20

"My dear brothers and sisters, take note of this: Everyone should be quick to listen, slow to speak and slow to become angry, because human anger does not produce the righteousness that God desires."

Bible Verse Reflection 2

Psalm 32:8

"I will instruct you and teach you in the way you should go; I will counsel you with my loving eye on you."

Reflect & Express

R This prayer and associated bible verses have opened my heart to be grateful for...

_____
_____
_____
_____
_____
_____
_____

E You have shown me through this prayer and bible verses that...

_____
_____
_____
_____
_____
_____
_____
_____

Act & Praise

A I pray for my grandchildren and myself to...

P I know Your Divine will is manifest, and my prayers are answered. I praise and give thanks for.... (write and state each prayer above as an affirmation)

Week 42 Prayer

Inspired Prayer

Divine Creator,

Open my heart, mind, eyes, and ears to Your presence. Guide me, Lord, in Your Name, Your Son Jesus' Name, and the Holy Spirit, as I pray for my grandchildren.

Grant them the grace to embrace forgiveness. Please help them forgive themselves for their mistakes and release guilt.

Teach them to extend forgiveness to others, especially when they feel frustrated or angry. And the ability to see Your grace, love, and life's lessons on the other side of forgiveness.

Show them forgiveness is the path to humility, to walking in Jesus' footsteps, and to being their true selves while allowing others the same freedom.

Thank You for watching over my grandchildren, for loving them, and for seeing the world through their beautiful eyes.

Send my love to them—let my light, peace, and presence be with them, as You are always with them.

With all my love and light,

Amen

Week 42 Bible Verses

Bible Verse Reflection 1

Colossians 3:12-14

"Therefore, as God's chosen people, holy and dearly loved, clothe yourselves with compassion, kindness, humility, gentleness and patience. Bear with each other and forgive one another if any of you has a grievance against someone. Forgive as the Lord forgave you. And over all these virtues put on love, which binds them all together in perfect unity."

Bible Verse Reflection 2

1 Peter 5:5

"In the same way, you who are younger, submit yourselves to your elders. All of you, clothe yourselves with humility toward one another, because, 'God opposes the proud but shows favor to the humble.'"

Reflect & Express

R This prayer and associated bible verses have opened my heart to be grateful for...

E You have shown me through this prayer and bible verses that...

Act & Praise

A I pray for my grandchildren and myself to...

P I know Your Divine will is manifest, and my prayers are answered. I praise and give thanks for.... (write and state each prayer above as an affirmation)

Week 43 Prayer

Inspired Prayer

Divine Creator,

We open our hearts, minds, eyes, and voices to Your grace, peace, and presence.

Guide my grandchildren and me toward what ignites their hearts and inspires their lives. Let them be immersed in the energy of Your love, giving them the strength and joy of angels on Earth.

In challenges and questions, may they find inspiration in Your energy. Help them to see Your perfection amidst imperfections and to choose grace and peace. Deepen their understanding of Your ever-present love. Illuminate their souls, Lord.

I am grateful for the moments spent witnessing their joy, sharing their laughter, and supporting them in frustration.

My deepest wish is that they live their best lives, embracing their true selves and fulfilling Your purpose.

I pray in Your Name, Your Son Jesus Christ's name, and the spirit of Your presence in our world.

Amen

Week 43 Bible Verses

Bible Verse Reflection 1

1 John 4:16

"And so we know and rely on the love God has for us. God is love. Whoever lives in love lives in God, and God in them."

Bible Verse Reflection 2

Romans 5:8

"But God demonstrates his own love for us in this: While we were still sinners, Christ died for us."

Reflect & Express

R This prayer and associated bible verses have opened my heart to be grateful for...

E You have shown me through this prayer and bible verses that...

Act & Praise

A   I pray for my grandchildren and myself to...

P   I know Your Divine will is manifest, and my prayers are answered. I praise and give thanks for.... (write and state each prayer above as an affirmation)

Week 44 Prayer

Inspired Prayer

Heavenly Creator,

I open my heart, mind, and being to Your presence.

Today, I've been reflecting on our tendency to judge ourselves harshly. It's vital to release these judgments and trust in Your guidance. Help us to see the best in ourselves and find Your reflection within us, especially in moments of self-doubt or criticism.

I pray for my grandchildren when they encounter feelings of shame, anger, failure, or even have a difficult day; they may find the strength to pause, breathe, and surrender these burdens to You. May they learn not to judge themselves harshly but to seek Your love and understanding in all situations.

I also pray for their parents and caretakers that they may recognize and nurture this Divine light within my grandchildren. Grant them the wisdom to provide opportunities for reflection, to seek You in every challenge, and to understand the truth in every situation.

Lord, I know beyond anger, fear, shame, and life's challenges there is always Your enduring presence. You offer us something greater: a deeper understanding of ourselves and a stronger connection with You.

Amen

Week 44 Bible Verses

Bible Verse Reflection 1

3 John 1:4

"I have no greater joy than to hear that my children are walking in the truth."

Bible Verse Reflection 2

Galatians 2:20

"I have been crucified with Christ and I no longer live, but Christ lives in me. The life I now live in the body, I live by faith in the Son of God, who loved me and gave himself for me."

Reflect & Express

R This prayer and associated bible verses have opened my heart to be grateful for…

_____
_____
_____
_____
_____
_____
_____

E You have shown me through this prayer and bible verses that…

_____
_____
_____
_____
_____
_____
_____
_____

Act & Praise

A I pray for my grandchildren and myself to...

P I know Your Divine will is manifest, and my prayers are answered. I praise and give thanks for.... (write and state each prayer above as an affirmation)

"Trust Your intuition. Divine Wisdom lies within."

Julie McDonnell

Wisdom & Purpose

Week 45 Prayer

Inspired Prayer

Divine Creator,

I call upon You for help and guidance to illuminate the unseen, unheard, and unloved aspects within my grandchildren.

Lord, may You fill these voids with Your radiant light, boundless love, and profound wisdom.

Let them know they are whole and complete in Your presence.

I pray every cell of their being is infused with Your grace, love, and acceptance, allowing them to radiate joy through their eyes and smiles, impacting all around them.

May they shine brightly in this world, embodying the kindness You have bestowed them.

Guide their hearts, ears, eyes, and minds to remain perpetually open to You.

Empower them to be pioneers of a new world where love for one another mirrors Your love for us.

Amen

Week 45 Bible Verses

Bible Verse Reflection 1

1 John 4:7-8

"Dear friends, let us love one another, for love comes from God. Everyone who loves has been born of God and knows God. Whoever does not love does not know God, because God is love."

Bible Verse Reflection 2

1 Peter 2:9

"But you are a chosen people, a royal priesthood, a holy nation, God's special possession, that you may declare the praises of him who called you out of darkness into his wonderful light."

Reflect & Express

R This prayer and associated bible verses have opened my heart to be grateful for...

_____
_____
_____
_____
_____
_____
_____

E You have shown me through this prayer and bible verses that...

_____
_____
_____
_____
_____
_____
_____
_____

Act & Praise

A I pray for my grandchildren and myself to...

P I know Your Divine will is manifest, and my prayers are answered. I praise and give thanks for.... (write and state each prayer above as an affirmation)

Week 46 Prayer

Inspired Prayer

Heavenly Creator and all that is love,

Let me be fully present in this moment.

Your constant presence, cradling my heart and patiently waiting for our time together, is a profound gift. I recognize and cherish this, and it's a treasure I yearn to share with others, especially my beloved grandchildren.

I wish for them to experience the freedom of choosing You in every moment. May they be enlightened by the emotional light You provide and feel the depth of Your unconditional acceptance.

Your love has no boundaries, and I pray this realization becomes a part of their consciousness. May they see it, feel it, know it, live it, and breathe it.

My prayer extends to the unimaginable doorways of understanding love, its depths, and how it can be expressed. May this understanding resonate through their lives, bringing joy and a sense of living fully.

I offer this prayer in Your name, Father, in Jesus' name, and in the Holy Spirit.

Amen

Week 46 Bible Verses

Bible Verse Reflection 1

Deuteronomy 30:19-20

"This day I call the heavens and the earth as witnesses against you that I have set before you life and death, blessings and curses. Now choose life, so that you and your children may live and that you may love the Lord your God, listen to his voice, and hold fast to him. For the Lord is your life, and he will give you many years in the land he swore to give to your fathers, Abraham, Isaac and Jacob."

Bible Verse Reflection 2

Ephesians 3:17-19

"So that Christ may dwell in your hearts through faith. And I pray that you, being rooted and established in love, may have power, together with all the Lord's holy people, to grasp how wide and long and high and deep is the love of Christ."

Reflect & Express

R This prayer and associated bible verses have opened my heart to be grateful for…

E You have shown me through this prayer and bible verses that…

Act & Praise

A I pray for my grandchildren and myself to...

P I know Your Divine will is manifest, and my prayers are answered. I praise and give thanks for.... (write and state each prayer above as an affirmation)

Week 47 Prayer

Inspired Prayer

Divine Creator,

I open my heart, mind, and being to You in all that is. Lord, graciously fill me with Your grace.

Illuminate these precious grandchildren with Your light, Lord. May they experience Your peace, love, and grace. Let these Divine gifts flow through them as they play, learn, laugh, and connect, embodying the joy of Your creation.

Instill in them an inner knowing, Lord, that they are part of Your Divine plan. Through their eyes, let us witness the world anew - with wonder, excitement, and joy in every smile, dance, and movement.

They are Your children, Lord. Keep them intimately connected to You. Bless them with the gift of sight to recognize Your presence, the wisdom to hear Your voice, and the comfort of Your calming presence when life challenges them.

Lord, let them recognize the signs of Your presence - love, acceptance, grace, peace, and forgiveness. With this knowledge and connection, ensure they always feel safe, make choices that honor You, and freely express their true selves.

Their impact on the world will be profound, guided by Your hand. I thank You with all of my heart, Lord,

Amen

Week 47 Bible Verses

Bible Verse Reflection 1

Matthew 19:14

"Jesus said, 'Let the little children come to me, and do not hinder them, for the kingdom of heaven belongs to such as these.'"

Bible Verse Reflection 2

John 10:27

"My sheep listen to my voice; I know them, and they follow me."

Reflect & Express

R This prayer and associated bible verses have opened my heart to be grateful for...

E You have shown me through this prayer and bible verses that...

Act & Praise

A I pray for my grandchildren and myself to...

P I know Your Divine will is manifest, and my prayers are answered. I praise and give thanks for.... (write and state each prayer above as an affirmation)

Week 48 Prayer

Inspired Prayer

Heavenly Creator,

Infuse my grandchildren's bodies with Your light, wisdom, and peace, revealing the essence of who they are and the purpose for which You created them.

Grant them, Lord, the insight to recognize and embrace the unique gifts they are meant to bring to this earth. Let them see, know, and embody Your Divine plan throughout childhood and adulthood.

Empower them to spread Your light, love, and grace around the world in the ways You deem fit. We often lose our way, Lord, searching for our identity, yet the truth resides solely in You. You alone replenish our inner being. You understand our creation's purpose and the glory we, as Your children, can manifest on this earth.

I am profoundly grateful, Lord, for this understanding, enabling me to share these truths with them. I trust in Your constant presence, guiding and holding their hands, reflecting the light, presence, and glory inherent in these precious souls.

With all my love and light, in this moment and always, I offer this prayer in Your Name, Your Son Jesus Christ's Name, and the Holy Spirit.

Amen

Week 48 Bible Verses

Bible Verse Reflection 1

James 1:5

"If any of you lacks wisdom, you should ask God, who gives generously to all without finding fault, and it will be given to you."

Bible Verse Reflection 2

Psalm 90:12

"Teach us to number our days, that we may gain a heart of wisdom."

Reflect & Express

R This prayer and associated bible verses have opened my heart to be grateful for...

E You have shown me through this prayer and bible verses that...

Act & Praise

A I pray for my grandchildren and myself to...

P I know Your Divine will is manifest, and my prayers are answered. I praise and give thanks for.... (write and state each prayer above as an affirmation)

Week 49 Prayer

Inspired Prayer

Divine Creator,

Open my heart, mind, and being to Your presence. Let my eyes and ears be attuned to You in my hopes and desires for my grandchildren.

I pray for their potential to be unlocked. May they find love and peace within themselves and recognize Your immense love for them.

Help them discover their true selves—gifts, joy, and vibrancy. I see Your light in their laughter, joy, and delight in simple things.

Lord, nurture these qualities. Grant them ease, flow, and resilience. Guide them through life's challenges, knowing Your presence provides strength to traverse hills and valleys.

I thank You for Your grace, forgiveness, and boundless love. Thank You for blessing these grandchildren with the opportunity to grow, express love, and shine their unique light in the world.

May their presence aid in healing our world, day by day.

With all my love and light, I send this prayer, trusting in Your eternal guidance.

Amen

Week 49 Bible Verses

Bible Verse Reflection 1

Psalm 51:10

"Create in me a pure heart, O God, and renew a steadfast spirit within me."

Bible Verse Reflection 2

Matthew 5:14-16

"You are the light of the world. A town built on a hill cannot be hidden. Neither do people light a lamp and put it under a bowl. Instead they put it on its stand, and it gives light to everyone in the house. In the same way, let your light shine before others, that they may see your good deeds and glorify your Father in heaven."

Reflect & Express

R This prayer and associated bible verses have opened my heart to be grateful for...

_____
_____
_____
_____
_____
_____
_____
_____

E You have shown me through this prayer and bible verses that...

_____
_____
_____
_____
_____
_____
_____
_____

Act & Praise

A I pray for my grandchildren and myself to…

P I know Your Divine will is manifest, and my prayers are answered. I praise and give thanks for…. (write and state each prayer above as an affirmation)

Week 50 Prayer

Inspired Prayer

Heavenly Creator and all that is the Great I AM,

I ask You to open my eyes, ears, heart, and mind, infusing every cell of my being with Your Divine presence. Ignite the Holy Spirit within me.

May Your grace, peace, and love permeate my being. Guide me to sense Your presence in the laughter and joy of my grandchildren. In their smiles and play, I witness Your spirit. And in their tears and frustration, I see Your comforting embrace.

Bestow upon them, O Lord, Your grace and profound wisdom. Though they may struggle to express or fully grasp it, instill in their tender hearts the serene assurance only You can provide.

Let them see themselves through Your eyes: flawless and cherished. Life will pose challenges, and they will encounter both failures and successes. I know they will also experience love and loss — as is the way of life. Through it all, teach them to seek and recognize You, even in moments of doubt and hardship.

Grant me the ability to convey to them a sense of certainty in Your ever-present support, the nurturing care You offer, and the complete acceptance of their innate beauty.

Amen

Week 50 Bible Verses

Bible Verse Reflection 1

Psalm 8:3-4

"When I consider Your heavens, the work of Your fingers, the moon and the stars, which you have set in place, what is mankind that you are mindful of them, human beings that you care for them?"

Bible Verse Reflection 2

Romans 5:3-5

"Not only so, but we also glory in our sufferings, because we know that suffering produces perseverance; perseverance, character; and character, hope. And hope does not put us to shame, because God's love has been poured out into our hearts through the Holy Spirit, who has been given to us."

Reflect & Express

R This prayer and associated bible verses have opened my heart to be grateful for...

E You have shown me through this prayer and bible verses that...

Act & Praise

A   I pray for my grandchildren and myself to...

P   I know Your Divine will is manifest, and my prayers are answered. I praise and give thanks for.... (write and state each prayer above as an affirmation)

Week 51 Prayer

Inspired Prayer

Divine Creator, the embodiment of love in all creation,

Open my heart, mind, and being to all the works of my hands.

Bless these precious moments with my grandchildren, for in their laughter, I see Your joy. Let me be a witness for them to Your grace, Your peace, Your wisdom.

May they feel Your love and peace through my presence, and let my life on this earth mirror Your compassion.

In my embrace, let them feel no judgment, only love—a sanctuary where they are wholly seen and deeply valued. Grant that my life is humble and true, and my actions guide their young hearts in Your ways.

Cultivate in them the strength to renounce judgment, to perceive Your presence in every trial.

With all my love, all my light, in this sacred moment and forever,

I pray in Your name, in Jesus' name, in the Holy Spirit, and in all that is Divine.

Amen

Week 51 Bible Verses

Bible Verse Reflection 1

Proverbs 3:13-18

"Blessed are those who find wisdom, those who gain understanding, for she is more profitable than silver and yields better returns than gold. She is more precious than rubies; nothing you desire can compare with her. Long life is in her right hand; in her left hand are riches and honor. Her ways are pleasant ways, and all her paths are peace."

Bible Verse Reflection 2

Hebrews 4:16

"Let us then approach God's throne of grace with confidence, so that we may receive mercy and find grace to help us in our time of need."

Reflect & Express

R This prayer and associated bible verses have opened my heart to be grateful for...

E You have shown me through this prayer and bible verses that...

Act & Praise

A I pray for my grandchildren and myself to...

P I know Your Divine will is manifest, and my prayers are answered. I praise and give thanks for.... (write and state each prayer above as an affirmation)

Week 52 Prayer

Inspired Prayer

Heavenly Creator, the embodiment of all that is Divine,

I seek guidance in Your love, light, peace, and presence.

I pray for my grandchildren today that they may experience Your Divine patience when frustrations arise or they are harsh on themselves for imperfections.

Grant them the wisdom to pause, take a breath, and practice self-compassion.

May they view each challenge as a journey--a path to express more of themselves and, ultimately, a way to discover You in every moment and find love in every challenge.

Empower them with the strength to confront any darkness, with the assurance You are ever-present. As they move forward with grace and patience, may they find You awaiting them.

With all of my love, light, peace, and patience, I offer this prayer in Your Name, Lord, in the Name of Jesus, in the Holy Spirit,

Amen

Week 52 Bible Verses

Bible Verse Reflection 1

James 1:2-4

"Consider it pure joy, my brothers and sisters, whenever you face trials of many kinds, because you know that the testing of your faith produces perseverance. Let perseverance finish its work so that you may be mature and complete, not lacking anything."

Bible Verse Reflection 2

Matthew 7:7

"Ask and it will be given to you; seek and you will find; knock and the door will be opened to you."

Reflect & Express

R This prayer and associated bible verses have opened my heart to be grateful for...

_____
_____
_____
_____
_____
_____
_____

E You have shown me through this prayer and bible verses that...

_____
_____
_____
_____
_____
_____
_____
_____
_____
_____

Act & Praise

A   I pray for my grandchildren and myself to...

P   I know Your Divine will is manifest, and my prayers are answered. I praise and give thanks for.... (write and state each prayer above as an affirmation)

"Prayer is essential to a healthy and vibrant relationship with God."

Jeffrey McDonnell

My Prayers

My Prayers

Date: _____

_____
_____
_____
_____

Date Manifested: _____

Personal Note: _____
_____

Date: _____

_____
_____
_____
_____

Date Manifested: _____

Personal Note: _____
_____

My Prayers

Date: _____

_____
_____
_____
_____

Date Manifested: _____

Personal Note: _____

_____

Date: _____

_____
_____
_____
_____

Date Manifested: _____

Personal Note: _____

_____

My Prayers

Date: _____

_____
_____
_____

Date Manifested: _____

Personal Note: _____
_____

Date: _____

_____
_____
_____

Date Manifested: _____

Personal Note: _____
_____

My Prayers

Date: _____

_____
_____
_____
_____

Date Manifested: _____

Personal Note: _____

_____

Date: _____

_____
_____
_____
_____

Date Manifested: _____

Personal Note: _____

_____

My Prayers

Date: _____

_____
_____
_____
_____

Date Manifested: _____

Personal Note: _____
_____

Date: _____

_____
_____
_____
_____

Date Manifested: _____

Personal Note: _____
_____

My Prayers

Date: _____

_____
_____
_____
_____

Date Manifested: _____

Personal Note: _____

_____

Date: _____

_____
_____
_____
_____

Date Manifested: _____

Personal Note: _____

_____

My Prayers

Date: _____

_____
_____
_____
_____

Date Manifested: _____

Personal Note: _____
_____

Date: _____

_____
_____
_____
_____

Date Manifested: _____

Personal Note: _____
_____

My Prayers

Date: _____

_____
_____
_____
_____

Date Manifested: _____

Personal Note: _____

_____

Date: _____

_____
_____
_____
_____

Date Manifested: _____

Personal Note: _____

_____

My Prayers

Date: _____

_____

_____

_____

_____

Date Manifested: _____

Personal Note: _____

_____

Date: _____

_____

_____

_____

_____

Date Manifested: _____

Personal Note: _____

_____

My Prayers

Date: _____

_____
_____
_____

Date Manifested: _____

Personal Note: _____

_____

Date: _____

_____
_____
_____

Date Manifested: _____

Personal Note: _____

_____

About the Authors

Julie and Jeffrey McDonnell are intuitives, teachers, and authors dedicated to faith and family. Jeffrey is a trained energy healer and former COO of Eden Method, who works with individuals and organizations to heal, grow, and reach their fullest potential.

Julie (EdD) is an accomplished retired elementary teacher and administrator who has taken time in this new phase of her life to embrace an ever-evolving spiritual journey while spending quality time with the grandchildren as a caregiver during their formative years. With a strong belief in the transformative power of prayer, they have come together to create this wonderful and uplifting 52-week journal for you to enjoy.

Family lies at the heart of Jeffrey and Julie's journey. As proud parents of two adult children, Jessica and Ciara, and loving grandparents to two beautiful souls, Nadia and Callan, they find their greatest joy in spending time with family. Jeffrey is affectionately known to their cherished grandkids as "PopPop," while Julie is lovingly referred to as "Mimi."

A deeply personal and painful experience marked their path to writing this book. When their granddaughter Camille, Nadia's twin sister, was lost during the final stages of their daughter Jessica's pregnancy, Jeffrey and Julie turned to prayer to navigate the profound pain, hurt, and trauma. Amid their grief, they discovered a remarkable source of solace and strength in their faith and the consistent practice of prayer.

Through this challenging journey, they felt a Divine calling to open their hearts and share this sacred space of prayer with others. Camille, their perfect Angel, had left an indelible mark on their lives, and they were determined to honor her memory by helping others find peace and connection through prayer.

Jeffrey, guided by a profound connection with Jesus, channeled his deep spirituality into crafting the prayers included in this 52-week journal. Jeffrey & Julie's mission is to support grandparents worldwide through a deeper connection with their grandchildren, nurturing them in faith, love, and prosperity.

Jeffrey and Julie have created this Journal through their shared commitment to faith, family, and the incredible power of prayer. This Journal is a testament to their unwavering love for their grandchildren and a beacon of hope for all who seek comfort and healing through prayer. Their story is one of resilience, love, and the enduring strength of the human spirit, fueled by faith in a higher power and the boundless love of family.

Upcoming Books & How to Connect With Us

Prayer Journals Release Dates in 2024 & 2025

Prayer Journal for Those Experiencing Anxiety & Depression (September 2024)

Prayer Journal for Those Experiencing Grief & Loss (November 2024)

Prayer Journal for the Sick & In Need of Healing (January 2025)

Prayer Journal for an Unborn Child (March 2025)

Spiritual Books Release Dates in 2025 & 2026

Power of Prayer (June 2025)

Divine Relationship (Dec 2025)

The Perfect Soul (June 2026)

To sign up for notifications or to learn more about these upcoming books, please go to **https://ourcoollife.com** or email us at support@ourcoollife.com.

Join the **Our COOL Life** community at **https://ourcoollife.com**, where you can interact with us and others directly in a private community.

Made in the USA
Monee, IL
02 September 2024